Faithing It

Faithing It

BRINGING PURPOSE BACK TO YOUR LIFE!

Cora Jakes
COLEMAN

DEDICATION

I dedicate this to every faither, to my family, to my
friends, to my followers, to my leaders. I dedicate this to
Nehemiah. I dedicate this to God, for without Him
I do not know what faithing it truly means!

Peace, Love, and Faithing It

Your Sister, Your Friend, Your Family, Your Leader

Cora Jakes Coleman

All photos used by permission

DESTINY IMAGE® PUBLISHERS, INC.
P.O. Box 310, Shippensburg, PA 17257-0310

"Promoting Inspired Lives."

This book and all other Destiny Image and Destiny Image Fiction books are available at Christian bookstores and distributors worldwide.

Front cover and interior design by: Koechel Peterson & Associates

Dust jacket design by: Eileen Rockwell

For more information on foreign distributors, call 717-532-3040.

Reach us on the Internet: www.destinyimage.com.

ISBN 13 HC: 978-0-7684-0789-1

ISBN 13 eBook: 978-0-7684-0790-7

For Worldwide Distribution, Printed in the U.S.A.

1 2 3 4 5 6 7 8 / 19 18 17 16 15

TABLE OF CONTENTS

Faithing It

FOREWORD
T.D. JAKES SR.

My daughter directs our children's ministry. She is in charge of helping us reach the young minds and hearts that attend our church. The irony of it all is that it was only yesterday she was the student and not the director, the child and not the parent. Whatever she did in between it was always done in church. Right or wrong, weak or strong, church is all she has ever known. She is the progenitor of my anointing, the epitome of my expectation. Cora is on a path with destiny that cannot be aborted.

The body of Christ welcomes a handmaiden whose journey though many tumultuous times and heart-breaking disappointments, has been crafted and designed to minister from a place of both experience and example in shaping a narrative for the souls of men. To say she is a jewel is an understatement. In fact not even an ultrasound would show you how vast and infinite her heart opens to those who need and hurt. I've watched her grow and explore, evolve and increase in wisdom and stature all in anticipation of this moment of impact to her generation and my own.

As witty as a comedian, as prayerful as a church mother, she wields a precocious ability and sobriety beyond her years. To be sure, Cora is an intricate mixture of contemporary ministry and old-school prayer. Her refreshing humor and unexpected wisdom will take you to a new place that will bless your life. As her father, both her mother and I, walked her through the perils of adolescence, a journey filled with nearly escaped mayhem and adventure. As arduous and daunting a task as it was, no commendation or human accolade awards us as parents like the validation of watching her evolve. She is a consummate mother, a devoted wife, and a daughter of the King.

Her flames of faith were ignited in part through the disappointments of being denied the birth of children. All she wanted in her whole life was children. Every time the headlines showed a baby discarded in a dumpster by an uncaring mother, we wept for her. She rode through the endless tests, medicines, and process of infertility clinic after clinic, desperately seeking her children. Little did we know that her excruciatingly painful journey of disappointment only helped to reveal that she would birth not through her womb, but through her words, a generation of Kingdom kids far beyond her wildest dreams. I've seen her adopt children both spiritually and naturally and bring vagrants inside out of the cold. I've watched her when she fed others at her own expense (and many times at mine) from near and far away.

She was the child who would bring anybody from anywhere into our home and into our lives, leaving us scrambling to prepare for the unexpected beneficiaries of her loving heart! Anything we gave her, she would likely give to one of her friends who needed something. Raising her increased my prayer life and decreased my finances as she thought we could feed the neighborhood and fix almost anyone she met that day from the grocery store to the gas station and almost nearly anywhere!

I want to share a story that occurred when she was still in diapers. I took her to see the doctor who, after careful examination, advised me I would need to admit her into the hospital due to a severe case of meningitis. I could hardly see the road as I drove first to my mother's house (for moral support) and then to tell my wife, her mother, that our first daughter was infirmed enough to be admitted. My mother and I faced her mother with the disturbing news, trying to explain that our daughter was going to need to go immediately to the hospital that day. As young parents we were both mortified. Minutes seemed like hours and hours seemed like days as we went through procedure after procedure. Her arm ended up bruised and swollen through misplaced IVs, and her brain ended up swollen from an improperly executed procedure. It seemed like everything that could go wrong, did. Finally, with much prayer and deep travail, we overcame and brought our baby home to lay on my chest as she did at that age, listening to my heartbeat for a rhythm that eventually and usually lulled her into a relaxed state of being and sleep that we all desired! It would be years before I realized that like the decree on the life of Moses, satan's fury against our child was in all actuality fear of what she has now become.

Today out of the ashes of despair she now rises to teach lessons on faith that have been sprinkled throughout her entire life! If you have ever faced a challenge for which your circumstances made you wonder if you could survive, this book is for you. If you have a faith that needs to be managed, massaged, or has been maligned by disappointing news and bleak conditions that defied human rectification, here's an answer coming through the pages ahead. It is no surprise that a child that was on the enemy's "hit list" from the beginning would find her inaugural literary work to be so rightly called *Faithing It*.

When she was born we were barely getting by, struggling to survive, we were literally on the verge of homelessness. Yet in that environment that was riddled with repossessed cars and often less than nutritious meals, she was born and raised. She watched her mother and I pull our family from the brink of annihilation to the basking light of promises attained. In short she has nursed on the breast milk of struggle, been fed on the tears of pilfering parents who were on the brink of bankruptcy, and finally wrapped in the rewards of a committed life to Jesus Christ, we reported complete and total victory! Health? Restored. Finances? Reclaimed. Family intact! We made it here by faith!

Now I see what the fight was about. It wasn't a battle against me. It wasn't a battle against her. It was the reckless fear coming from the defeated foe whose tactics were derelict in their intent to stop her from reaching you. Her message is a faith-building, courageous commitment to help you bridge the gulf between the circumstances you face and the future you are destined to attain. With all the pride of an effusive father, who marches his daughter down the aisle to her beloved, I hand this book to you. As her father, I am just a voice crying in the wilderness. I've come to say to you to prepare your heart and mind. She has processed to this point to turn misery to ministry. This is the moment where I pass her power and pain off into your hands with the intent that when you have finished reading her thoughts, you will attain a deeper sense of purpose.

Ladies and Gentlemen, brothers and sisters, I introduce to some and present to others, my daughter, and God's servant, Cora Brionne Jakes-Coleman. Receive her and the mustard seed faith she brings to your garden of thought. The next words you read will come from Cora. Receive her words as she plants the thoughts that will enable you to go beyond making it to Faithing IT!

PREFACE

People often ask me what it's like to live with someone who's famous. I tell them, "It's like this. By the time I turned eight years old, my name was officially 'Bishop Jakes' daughter.'" Not that being T. D. Jakes' daughter is a bad thing, but suddenly my personal identity as Cora Jakes was a thing of the past, and I had a front-row seat in the "fish bowl" life of a high-profile preacher.

No pressure, right? Wrong! There was admittedly an undeniable pressure to become something more than a little girl who dreamed of being a mother, playing with baby dolls, and wearing Mickey Mouse afro puffs in West Virginia. In the midst of trying to establish and maintain my identity, we relocated to Texas—which felt like being thrown into a museum!

Now, I can't tell you my whole life's story in this little preface, but I will share more as we unpack this concept of "faithing it" together throughout this book.

I *can* tell you that I figured out pretty quickly that trying to be "normal" in the family fish bowl was not going to be an easy task, but that did not stop me from trying. And it didn't stop my partners in crime either—my siblings.

We learned from our parents that families stick together. Jamar, Jermaine, Dexter, Sarah, and I grew up being watched by the world. The fact that we were under constant scrutiny only drew us closer. As the children of a famous preacher/celebrity (take your pick) we were overwhelmed. There was so much pressure to get everything right and certainly never make a mistake. We learned how to hold our heads up high even when our feet were trembling from the world falling apart beneath us. We figured out how to be strong at our weakest moments and, sadly, we learned that not everyone is your friend and means you well. Some people are simply around as vultures, just waiting to scrutinize you…just like patrons in a museum.

As I grew older, I did eventually make trustworthy friends and I developed a deep compassion for people. I still dreamed of being a mom, and the desire to take care of children only grew inside my heart. But as innocent as my life was on the surface, I was secretly going through an emotional hurt.

At the age of ten years old, I was molested by a young boy in a bathroom stall at my elementary school. It was heartbreaking for me. I knew this boy, and I trusted him. After being violated by someone I trusted, I understood for the first time that life was not always going to be easy and I wasn't exempt from hard times. For a long time I rehearsed all the things I did wrong. It was not until several years later that I accepted that I was a victim of circumstance, and there was nothing I could do about it.

I am typically a very strong person, but some things can shake you to the core. I can honestly say that it was through my relationship with Christ that I overcame this trauma. Even as a little girl, I knew I was called to be something bigger than what I could see at the time. Mind you, I have always known that with great privilege in life you will have great obstacles, but as a young girl I didn't realize how great some of those obstacles would be. I'm grateful that my parents taught me that with faith in God you can get through anything.

My life, purpose, and the promise of God came with great obstacles and heartbreak along the way—a series of circumstances that I will share later in this book. But I can tell you that those heartbreaks and storms forced me to develop a true faith in God. With maturity comes wisdom. As I grew older, I learned that I had to partner my faith with my fight, and it was at this point in my life that I developed a term I use called "faithing it."

"Faithing it" means that we must learn how to develop our faith and go after those obstacles with faith. You are a conqueror because you are faithing it. You are a fighter because you choose to be. You cannot get to great purpose, promise, and legacy without great tribulation, but you can trust that everything works together for good in God's timing.

You cannot get to great purpose, promise, and legacy without great tribulation.

Speaking of timing, you chose this day and this hour to read this page. I believe God's timing is at work right now, and it is my hope that when you turn the last page of this book you will go back into your life with a better understanding of who you are, why you are, and what your storms mean for your ultimate destiny and purpose in life. So are you ready to stand up and fight with me? "Get ready!"

Faithing It

INTRODUCTION

"Faithing it." What does that mean? It means that in order to get through our problems and bypass our circumstances, we must fight with faith—and without a faith fight there cannot be a win. Faith is obtained by God! If we choose to speak faith and fight obstacles with our faith, we cannot lose.

Are you in a struggle right now? I want you to know that you are not alone. God has you in His hand! You *will* make it, and I'm here to tell you that there is not just one way to win, but there are several ways to win.

I wrote this book because I love you, and I do not want you to feel alone or be alone. I want to be clear. Just because my earthly father is known as "the world's bishop," that doesn't mean that I am above you. I am coming to you as a friend and sister to encourage you to leap into your dream, purpose, and promise. My hope is that you walk away with a better understanding of who you are and what your struggles mean in connection to your ultimate destiny.

Before we begin this journey together, I want to tell you a story that I tell to audiences everywhere I speak. This story is really what led me to faithing it. This story is why I'm telling you to fight with faith for your purpose.

The "Accident"

I was twenty-two years old, engaged to the most wonderful man in the world, and thoroughly enjoying my work as a nanny and babysitter. One evening before going off to work, I told my mother that my hips and back hurt badly, but I wasn't sure why.

That night on the way home from the babysitting job, I was driving and talking to my fiancé on the speakerphone when my green arrow light came up to turn left. So I began to turn, and suddenly I looked up to headlights coming directly at me. I immediately prayed, "God, get me out of this." The truck rammed into me going 40 mph. My air bag burst in my face and glass shattered everywhere. My car caved in on me.

I was scared. This was the worst car accident I had ever been in. I remembered one thing. I prayed God would get me out of this. I believed God would get me out of this when the collision ended. I opened my eyes. My coat was burned from the airbag, and all I could hear was, "She's dead! She

Without a faith fight there cannot be a win.

has to be dead!" The fireman came running to my car, and I opened my car and stood up—without a visible bruise or scratch—nothing. I was just sore.

I didn't go to the emergency room that night. I went home that night asking God, why me? Why would You cause me to go through that? What was the purpose of this? I woke up very sore the next day. My mother took me to the doctor.

During the CAT scan at the doctor's office, they found a 7 cm cyst on one ovary and a 9 cm cyst on my other ovary. The doctor told me that I was days away from my fallopian tubes twisting and shutting down my reproductive system.

Why Me, God?

I was stunned. All I ever wanted to be was a mother. Everything that I dreamed about, everything I hoped for would have been impossible had it not been for a car hitting me at 40 mph. If the devil had his way I would have been dead, and everything that would allow me to produce would have been dead.

You may not know the why, but sometimes the hard things happen to us because we are being saved from the enemy destroying our ability to produce. Whether spiritual or natural, the enemy is after your seed. You may have just been hit hard and you may be in pain, but all of this is leading to your salvation.

God saved me in a unique way because God is a unique God and He has to orchestrate things accordingly. Had I not gone through the hurt, the soreness, and later the surgery, I would have been in a lot of trouble. Later, the surgeon discovered that one of the cysts was much larger than they originally thought, and because of that I would have to lose one of my fallopian tubes and one of my ovaries.

One hit by a car led to me to discovering two cysts, the loss of an ovary, the loss of a fallopian tube, and a news flash from the doctor that it wasn't probable for me to get pregnant without going through in vitro fertilization. Needless to say, I was devastated by the news. I saw the pain of the process, and I was hurt by the facts in front of me. I wanted to live in the "Why me, God?" but had I not gone through all that, I wouldn't have gotten to the great rewards of my life.

What's Your Story?

So what's your story? Do you have unanswered questions about the circumstances in your life? Are you wondering when your rewards are coming?

I want to invite you right now to join me in faithing it—fighting with your faith to produce purpose. If you decide to faith it, the enemy will not control your story, your win, or your life. This is *your* time to move forward with zeal, tenacity, and determination. This book is going to inspire you to believe God, and push you to stretch and develop the fighter in you.

Are you ready to stand up and faith it with me? I want you to know that I believe God's best is just ahead for both of us. Let's talk.

Faithing It

MY STORY

Faithing It

ONE

You Are God's Book— Respect the Process

You saw me before I was born. Every day of my life
was recorded in Your book. Every moment was
laid out before a single day had passed.

(PSALM 139:16 NLT)

God is the author of your story! Every good story has a multi-dimensional character who experiences inner struggles, outer conflicts, and a satisfying "aha moment" where everything finally comes together for that character. You can't go to a bookstore, pick up a book, tear out the happy parts that you like, and then move on. If you pick up that book and you want those eight pages that you like, then you will have to buy all the other pages. And to live a successful life in all the other chapters of your book, you're going to need to faith it to the last page! God is crafting a marvelous book about each one of us, and in order to get to complete wholeness we must first understand our life is a series of processes all built to create us into the person God wants us to be. Don't worry! Your "aha moment" is on the way!

I started dating my (now) husband, Brandon, six years ago and boy we were head over heels in love! When you are that in love, you have the tendency to want to move really quickly. Whenever we would feel the "urge" to move quickly, Brandon would look at me and say, "We have to respect the process." At the time, though, it was so difficult. Although I knew what he meant, I had to patiently realize that there was a process that had to be implemented in order for us to get to our ultimate goal. We loved each other and we were grown, but it was not a time for "urgencies" and we had to respect the process. I had to grow more, and he did too.

Don't worry! Your "aha moment" is on the way!

All great things come with a process. Was it hard for Brandon and me? Indeed! At first it was very hard, and then it became easy as God grew and matured us. We faced trials for sure and gained major perseverance, but at the end of the day it was our respect for our process that got us to our goal. Really, in all honesty, trusting God *is* the process. Allowing Him to lead you is the ultimate maturity.

You Can't Skip the Process

You have to understand that "the process" is a normal way of life. When you think about the basic things of life, there's a process. When you are getting ready to cook for your family, you pick something out, then you build a grocery list, and then you have to go get the groceries, and preheat the oven, and prepare your meal. The meal cannot come forth without a process, and if you do not go through the process your family will be hungry. Even when you are tired, working, and things are going crazy, you have to cook and you have to go to the grocery store. You cannot skip the process. No matter how easy the meal is, you cannot skip the process to get there.

When you are crying out to God for Him to do something and it does not come through, you wonder, *Lord, why are You blessing everyone else connected to me, but not blessing me?* It is in that very moment in the middle of your WHY that God is telling you to respect the process—"trust Me." It is in your maturity and completeness where you realize God is for you, and what He said He would fulfill, He will, but you must trust Him.

Our lives are living testaments of several processes both big and small. In our relationships of life there is a process. The point is, you can't run away from the process. You have to face it. If you want to be a wife, a husband, or even someone's significant other, you have to go through a process.

Being in a relationship you will have obstacles, ups and downs, but it's all a process in order to get you to your promise. God is asking you to face your process, face your trials, and when you can believe God in the midst of your trial, then, and only then, you will not lack anything. Your promise is in your problems. Those problems are there so you do not lack anything. God wants you to mature and become complete. Now when we look at "complete" I know that can be confusing, but it means that He wants you to be whole—He wants you to be full. The book of James tells us about the process that brings us to maturity:

*Consider it pure joy, my brothers and sisters, whenever you face trials of many kinds, because you know that the testing of your faith produces perseverance. Let perseverance finish its work so **that you may be mature and complete**, not lacking anything* (James 1:2-4 NIV).

It's all a process in order to get you to your promise.

Perseverance as defined on Google is "steadfastness in doing something despite difficulty or delay in achieving success." James 1 tells us that the testing of our faith will bring perseverance. So God was simply saying, yes, we will face trials, and yes, it is going to be hard. But the good news is that our current hardship is going to develop steadfastness in whatever we do, despite difficulty or delay in our leap of faith.

Are you looking for purpose? Chances are your purpose and your plan are right there in your face. Let me explain how this happened to me.

The Chapter in My Book that I Didn't Like

As I entered adulthood, I felt pretty steady and secure. I had realized one dream of working with children, and God loved me enough to allow me to meet the love of my life—an amazing man and artist, Brandon Coleman a.k.a. Skii (Sky) Ventura, and my life as far as I knew it was going great. Then I hit another obstacle. I mentioned in the introduction to this book the accident that I was in when Brandon and I were engaged to be married. Since that time, I've been in the fight of my life. I am currently dealing with the diagnosis that I will not get pregnant without fertility treatments due to PCOS (Polycystic Ovarian Syndrome). This very diagnosis is one of the reasons why I wrote this book.

After hearing such horrible news, right when we were ready to marry and start a family, I was heartbroken. I didn't like this chapter in my book at all! Yet again, here I was going through "everything that a young woman goes through." For years, I dreamed of becoming a mother, not to mention the fact that I had "mothered" countless children in my day care work and as the Children's Ministry Director of the Potter's House of Dallas. Now to hear I would not have children—I was disappointed beyond belief. But I did not let that stop me from trying, preparing, and getting ready to become a mother.

Often we let what the world says detour us from our desire and from what God said would happen. Then instead of even trying, we stop fighting altogether. Not me! I shook myself off and I looked for ways to make my dream come true. I became a mom to my beautiful daughter through adoption. I experienced the miracle of choosing my beautiful daughter. You don't have to birth a child in order to be a mom. With that being said, never make a backup plan for what God promised you. Keep the faith in the promise! When I was a little girl, I had a dream one night of being a mom to a son. I am holding on to the promise of my son from God, and I won't and can't stop faithing it until it comes to fruition.

You have to make up your mind to fight for your promise! The power is in your fight, so FIGHT FOR IT! You can do it.

Faithing It with Perseverance

God is developing your purpose through your trial, and it's likely that you are currently in the process—meaning a series of actions or steps taken in order to achieve a particular end. The process of life cannot come without perseverance. Beware! You can lose your promise when you do not match the two together. It is important that whatever you go through in life, you go through it with perseverance while faithing it for your promise.

Whenever I think of perseverance, I think of my favorite story in the Bible—Job (pronounced Jobe). Maybe you've heard someone say, "It's been a Job day." That means, "I am having an incredibly difficult day and everything that *could* go wrong, *did* go wrong!" Job was a man of God, and an entire book of the Bible is named after Job and is dedicated to his story. Let me tell you a little bit about Job!

You see, the Bible says Job was an upright man, and because of the greatness that he sought, he was chosen to go through great trials. How crazy is it that? We get chosen to go through great trials when we are Christians? What sense does that make to go through problems when you are a child of the King? What if I told you that you were chosen to go through trials because you are a child of the King seeking righteousness, and the enemy wants to destroy your promise and your ability to prosper?

Here's how it went down. Satan went to God in heaven to accuse the people on earth. (Satan still accuses God's people, even today.) When satan accused the people living on the earth during Job's day, God said to satan, "Have you considered My servant Job?"

Satan replied, "No wonder Job's so righteous. Look at that hedge of protection You've put around him! Take down that hedge and I'll get him to curse You" (see Job 1:8–11).

God allowed satan a limited access to Job, and Job lost everything but his life. He got sick, he was shaken, he was broken, yet he never once cursed God—although he did curse himself. There will be times in life when you wonder where God is, and He is standing right there, but He is taking you through the process in order to bless you. You must understand that the enemy is not hitting you without God's permission. You need to know that the importance of Job's story is that the enemy had to go before God before even touching Job. Your circumstance does not come without granted approval from the throne. It is also important to note that the enemy is not a creator—he is an imitator. If he attacked Job, then he will attack us, too. Whatever the enemy presents to you is just a reconstructed situation that he has used before.

Job's friends thought he was crazy. His wife turned against him and even tempted him to sin! She said, "Why don't you just curse God and die?" What a test! But Job still trusted God while he was in his process, and he never stopped believing in God.

You are designed by God to persevere. You are designed to face trials because you need them in

Whatever the enemy presents to you is just a reconstructed situation that he has used before.

29

order to get to the promise. Before you can get to what God has for you, you will have to face adversity.

Processes are not easy. Think about all of the conflict and struggles a main character goes through in a novel or even a movie. Those intense struggles make the "aha moment" even better! So keep faithing it, no matter where you are in your process.

From the Process to the Promise

Sometimes we have to process our mind, friends, and family before we can get to our promise. The overall point is this: Are you willing to go through the process in order to get to the thing God wants for you? Even if it means losing everything in order to gain more in the end?

Philippians 3:8 says, "Yet indeed I also count all things loss for the excellence of the knowledge of Christ Jesus my Lord, for whom I have suffered the loss of all things, and count them as rubbish, that I may gain Christ."

You see, there is much to gain! Not only will you obtain God's promises for your life, but you walk out of your process *knowing* Jesus!

Let's consider Jesus. Jesus was a carpenter. He created things, and He was a builder. Jesus was God in the flesh, and it's only natural that we will go through processes in life simply because Jesus was a builder. He was a carpenter, and carpenters know more than most that there is a process in everything that you want to create. They understand that you cannot make something without a process.

Step out of who you think you are and who people think you are, and begin to walk in what God spoke over you. And just in case you did not know who God said you are, then you need to just walk in the simple fact that you are a child of the King of kings. You are a child of a carpenter, and He is building you into something beautiful. Molded and created in His perfect image, you can walk in the fact that you are called to be great.

I believe that fighting and faith go hand in hand. That's what gets us through these obstacles—our ability to stand before the mountain with faith and a fight and command the mountain to move. It *will* move!

Every superhero has a villain, and every hero has a backstory.

God is molding you to be great. He is molding you to overcome. He is molding you into completion and maturity. You are not forgotten. You are worthy of your dreams and hopes. You are not being punished; you are being processed. You deserve to gain all God has for you. Do not limit yourself because the storms are raging, but look at the storm and say, "I will trust you, Lord." If you were not meant to be anything, you would not have trials to face. If you were not meant to be strong and great, then you would need no molding.

I wrote this book because I believe in you. As your sister in Christ, I am here to faith it with you so we can rise up together against the enemy and break his chains!

You are God's book, and right now, today, you are living out a page in that book. Is today's page overwhelming you? Do you feel alone in this chapter of your life? As your sister and friend, I want to tell you that it is through your hurt that you become a hero. Every superhero has a villain, and every hero has a backstory. Will you let me pray for you right now?

I pray that God give you the grace to endure the pain of the process. I pray that God open your eyes to see the people who are for you and the people who are not. I pray that God allow you to embrace this in a new way where you understand that your storms have been meant to make you grow stronger. I pray that God ignite the purpose and gifting inside of you, that you might be able to go after your purpose with everything that you have. I pray that faith be your encourager, that faith be your pusher, that faith be your strength, and that you begin to become a faither. I pray that you take on this challenge to become better than who you are, that you do not look behind you, and that you do not let the enemy keep you bound in the past, but that you challenge yourself to be even better than who you think you are supposed to be. I pray that you give God the ability to do great things in you. I pray you get something out of this journey, and that you understand that I am here for you, I am faithing with you, and, trust me, we are going to win and I pray you know that.

Scan this code for Cora's Chapter 1
PRAYER FOR YOU!

Or Visit
WWW.CORAJAKESCOLEMAN.COM

TWO

"Faithing It" Through the Chapter I'm in Now

For if you live according to the flesh you will die;
but if by the Spirit you put to death the deeds
of the body, you will live.

(ROMANS 8:13)

Who or what is the villain in your life's story? I'd be interested to know what came to your mind just now when I asked that question!

I think it can be extremely helpful to locate yourself where you are right now in the process to your promise. Sometimes our own emotional reactions to the storms of life can rise up to be the worst villain in our lives. I know from experience that our inner struggles can squeeze the life out of us if we allow them to hang on. Other times the obstacle in front of us looks impossible to move because it's so big.

Remember, every superhero has a villain, and every hero has a backstory. So let's locate ourselves and what process we are in right now in our backstory.

First, in every good book there is a beginning and an end. The pages in between represent the process we've been talking about. The best way to think about processes is stages. I believe that stages of grief are very similar to a cycle that we go through in the daily process of walking out God's promises.

Let me be clear about one thing. I believe that our flesh has to die by the end of this process. Let me talk about this for just a moment before we define the stages of grief.

You may wonder what I'm talking about—our flesh has to die. Well, it's important to understand that in order to gain purpose you have to be willing to sacrifice your own fleshly desires for God's will for your life. We must be willing to spiritually sacrifice within ourselves and kill those things that are not like God in order to reach our purpose. You are only as strong and as blessed as what you are willing to sacrifice to get it.

You have to be willing to sacrifice your own fleshly desires for God's will for your life.

> *For if you live according to the flesh you will die; but if by the Spirit you put to death the deeds of the body, you will live* (Romans 8:13).

Stages of Grief

Grief comes into play when we have to completely sacrifice ourselves so that God can use us in the end for His overall purpose and glory to be fulfilled. I believe that, like the stages of grief, our process may come in different orders and times in our lives, but at the end we've met each process.

The stages of grief are:

- Denial

- Isolation

- Anger

- Bargaining

- Depression

- Acceptance

Let's talk about it, and how my mind breaks each one down.

Denial

People go through levels of denial. First, we don't believe in ourselves. We may hear God speak to us about what is up ahead, but we can see our own weaknesses and think, I will never get there. I'm not good enough or smart enough or strong enough.

If we are in denial, then we will begin to isolate ourselves from everything and everyone.

Isolation

We isolate ourselves because we are afraid. First, we can be in denial and don't believe in ourselves. Second, if we were to surround ourselves with God's people, then God would use those people to speak inadvertently into our lives. Simply put, we are not ready for other people to believe in what God has for us, so we go through isolation.

The beauty of this stage is that it is in the various levels of our isolation when God speaks to us the most. You may find that the times you spend alone are the times when God begins to give you the most direction.

But there is a difference between healthy isolation and unhealthy isolation. Devotional time and isolation are not the same thing. Isolation that does not produce a stronger relationship with God is unhealthy isolation. But if your time away from the doubts, fear, and outside voices brings you closer to God and closer to believing His promises for your life, that is healthy isolation. The bottom line is that some form of isolation is experienced during your process, and that isolation will either lead you to success or oppression.

Anger

I explained earlier that our flesh has to die in order for us to truly live. That dying to flesh often doesn't feel good. Sometimes it angers us when we don't get results immediately or we assume that the sacrifice of our flesh doesn't matter to God. If we do not see God acknowledge our sacrifice in the time frame that we think that it should happen, then we have the audacity to get upset! It's at this point that we can be tempted to stop faithing it and either run away or go back into the world.

It's okay to be angry, but it's not okay to stop fighting.

We must lay hold of patience to be able to stand and wait for God to acknowledge us. Don't forget, my friend, that the reason we sacrificed our flesh to begin with was so that we could gain purpose, power, and our promise. You cannot get any of that without God! So we sacrifice our flesh to get something out of God's hand, and when He doesn't move as quickly as we want Him to, we get angry.

To this stage I say, "Get over yourself. You win because God fought before you got there." Think about this—God had to be patient with *you* to get you to sacrifice in the first place! So let me encourage you to be patient and wait for God's timing instead of getting angry in your own timing. Our anger comes because we want to make God do our will instead of trying to operate in God's will. When you can release yourself from your own expectations, then you release God to be able to work for you. Anger is a natural emotion, but it is not a healthy emotion if it is not producing a benefit to you.

It's okay to be angry, but it's not okay to stop fighting.

Bargaining

The next step in our process or grief stages is bargaining. I relate to bargaining so well—mostly during my wanting a husband (LOL). I found myself wanting to stop going through so much pain from bad experiences with past boyfriends, but I was in a process and God wanted to bring that pain to the forefront so He could heal me.

I can remember after accepting my call into ministry, I sacrificed my flesh for the better will of God to come forward. Right away I asked God, "Please, Lord, if You send me my husband right now, I promise I will appreciate him, and I will praise You in advance and even more when he comes. I know that You are able to do this for me!"

Now, when I accept God's call and His will, I cannot bargain with Him for my will and my desire. My hope is that as you read this right now, you will pray:

God let my will line up to Your will. And if my desires don't match Your desires for me, Lord, then help me to desire even more what matches Your will for my life.

We must understand that God has the best deal for us so we don't need to bargain with Him. Yes, sometimes He will place us in situations in life that will make us sad, and that we may not value, but His ways are higher than ours. If we choose to walk with Him and not bargain with Him, then we are already on a level of success in our walk that we may not have ever been able to reach before!

Depression

How you deal with this next stage is up to you. Truthfully, we all go through some point of depression in our process to success and purpose. Usually, we encounter depression at that moment of God's test when He asks, "Will you trust Me?" For Job, it was the moment when he cursed his own life.

There are different forms of depression that are associated with the stages of grief. One type is a response to the reality of the overall loss. Sadness and regret are the primary two things that drive that particular type of depression. You may question the cost of your sacrifice of flesh:

- What it will mean to go after my purpose?

- How will it impact the people around me, especially my family?

- Am I good enough to obtain this type of dream and purpose?

This is the time when you need to evaluate the people around you because, in that moment, when everything looks hopeless, you need someone to believe with you. You need friends and family members who will recognize your hope to become something bigger than your obstacle so that they can help to push you through.

Now the other type of depression isn't as obvious, and in some cases it is handled during the time of isolation. At this point, you find you have to let go of people or responsibilities that are holding you back from your purpose. It's the time when you have to truly accept that you have evaluated your friends and your surroundings, and God has told you who is for you and who isn't, and you have to accept that separation is necessary and you have to say good-bye. Let me tell you, it's not easy. But on the positive side, make sure that you find the people that you know are for you whether you are wrong, right, fail, or succeed. Just spend time with them and get affirmation and support from them.

Acceptance

Acceptance is my favorite stage. This stage is often overlooked and, ironically enough, it is the one that takes the longest to get to. Let's just look at the definition. *Acceptance* as defined in *Webster's* is "The act of accepting; the fact of being accepted." The reason I picked that definition is because we often have a hard time accepting that God has accepted, called, and chosen us.

Acceptance takes the longest time to get to because we then have to understand that we didn't sacrifice ourselves for nothing, and that God is going to use us even though we've made mistakes, even though we've handled some things in the wrong way. The act of accepting comes when you are able to accept the fact that it's okay to make mistakes, and God can still use you for something bigger than yourself.

The acceptance comes in when you realize the pain, depression, and anger are to benefit you, not break you—when you are able to understand that, the Bible says the enemy will come in like a flood and the weapons will form, but God will build a standard against it, and they won't prosper. It is your choice to either concentrate on the flood and the weapons or to focus on the standard God builds. When God builds the standard, the flood and weapons set against you will not prosper. Most of us are drowning in an invisible flood. It's easy to say that the storm will rage and there is power in your pain. The reality is the power is in your perspective.

I've walked through these stages of grief, and let me say that it has not been easy. After twenty-six years of living through heartbreak, struggles, problems, and tribulation, I can tell you that because of my life's journey, I know where God is taking me. I can only imagine where He is taking you. What has God spoken to you in times past? Whatever God has spoken to you, the fact that you decided to take this journey indicates it must be a pretty big deal indeed.

The power is in your perspective.

Don't Call It Quits!

You will go through the storm in order to develop your fight. You will go through the trials in order to develop your fight, and when you develop your fight then you must let that strength and that fight grow and finish in you. You must let your storm finish in order for you to mature and gain everything you are praying for. The beautiful thing about the Word of God is that when you truly spend time in the Scriptures it breaks down and you receive revelations about your placement in life that will truly wow you.

Are you about to call it quits? Don't do it! I believe in you. I believe God has greatness in store for you. I believe that God is molding you because you are great. The beautiful thing about diamonds is that they come from deep within the earth, from the bottom. Diamonds can also be found in water. I am calling out the diamond in you. Diamonds are created through massive amounts of pressure and heat. If the pressure is too low, the diamond cannot form. If the heat is not hot enough, the diamond can't form. Before it becomes a beautiful ring, that diamond goes through a series of cutting processes. Dare I say God is allowing you to be cut to shape your story into something beautiful?

God is bringing about clarity to your life right now as you read this. And this is step one to the beginning of your greatness. Please know that God is breaking you into something beautiful, and your purpose came with a process. There is beauty in your breaking, and I am here to tell you that if you respect the process, you can get to the promise.

One of the most difficult things about the process is that we usually don't know when the struggles and storms are going to stop. Most of us know when the beginning of our storm started. It is in that moment when your back is against the wall and everything is falling apart and you do not know what to do. The thing is, you can never know when it is going to end.

Can you imagine being in your Job stage? You are covered in boils, children died, friends turned away from you, your spouse tells you to curse God and die, and you do not have a clue when it is going to be over? The hardest part about the process is that you have to believe God and you have to hold God's hand even if you do not know where He is leading you or how long it's going to take to get there.

A few years ago I did a project in which I was blind for a day. I went out into the world without the ability to see, with only my friends to lead me, and that was the hardest part of the project. That was the day when I learned how God wants us to depend on Him. He wants us to be able to be led by Him even if we do not know where He is taking us. I had to learn that first. Step one of the process was to believe and be led by God. If you choose to take God's hand and walk with Him, He will get you through the other steps.

Your trials have come to make you complete. Job went through the trials and the problems and the hurt, but when he matured and became "complete," when he handed it all over to God, he got back more than he started with. Could it be that God is placing you in your Job process so that He can get you to your big promise? Are you being persecuted or hated like Job? Are you enduring loss or sickness like Job? This has powerful meaning because some people would look at that meaning and say, "Dang, that's awful!" But that definition is what *people* saw him as, and not what God saw him as.

God said, "Have you considered Job, that there is none like him on the earth, a blameless and upright man, one who fears God and shuns evil?" (Job 1:8). Job walked in what *God* said, not in what people said. The problem that we have is that we are walking in what people said and not in what God said. If you flipped that definition, you could go on to say that is what the devil felt about him.

The devil wanted to persecute Job and he hated him. You see, you have people in your life who are speaking things about you and defining who you are by where you are.

People's Opinion or God's Opinion?

Your trials have come to make you complete.

We need to get something straight. We are God's book, and He's not writing our book to impress the people around us! Furthermore, it is God who will get the glory on the last page of your book, not the devil! And God isn't trying to place us on the top-ten best seller list so we can outrank and outdo the people around us. We need to decide right here and now whose opinion matters to us the most—God's opinion or people's opinion?

You are God's book and He is writing His story about you right now. I am here to tell you that you are designed for such a time as this, and that God is for you. I know that at times it can seem like He does not hear you, and you are lost in the middle of this world. I want to remind you that God is fighting for you and, as long as you trust Him, then nothing can hurt you or be against you.

The Bible says in Romans 8:31, "What shall we say about such wonderful things as these? If God is for us, who can ever be against us?" The world cannot be against you, your friends cannot be against you, your family cannot be against you, even you cannot be against you! Nothing, I mean absolutely nothing, can be against you. You have to believe God that your circumstance is not your outcome, it is simply your process. Putting God ahead of your storm allows Him the opportunity to lead you out of it.

You need to stop allowing the people behind you to tell you who you are and look ahead of you where God is. Some of us need to place God ahead of us instead of trying to figure it out on our own. Your circumstances, both past and present, cannot define where you are called to go. Do not let where you are today hinder where God is trying to take you tomorrow.

Job tossed and turned. He battled and cursed his birth until he finally gave it to God—and that is when his process ended, and he lacked nothing. The timing of your process is not the same as everyone else's. God is seeking a different process for you. You must understand that if you start desiring where someone else is, then you will have to take on their process. You are not allowed to pick and choose what you want to have from someone else's blessings.

Your circumstance is not your outcome, it is simply your process.

You see, we get in a habit of fake rejoicing. You know what I mean. Someone gets something you have been praying for, and you clap, jump up and down, and you thank Jesus for them, but on the inside you are envious. On the inside you are breaking apart because you wish you had what they had. You say that and you stand there in your hurt and you do not realize that you can't pick and choose.

We All Face Trials

Let me make this simple. Jessica gets a job Ashley has been waiting for. Ashley graduated from college, has a great family, and loves the Lord. Ashley says to Jessica, "Oh, that is wonderful." She is happy for Jessica, but on the inside she is jealous of Jessica's blessing.

Ashley does not realize Jessica was beaten all her life by her parents, has tried to kill herself several times, is struggling with a crack addiction, got the job by the skin of her teeth, and if she did not get the job she would be evicted from her apartment. Ashley just saw Jessica's job offer and immediately wanted to be in Jessica's position, but if she took the job she must also take Jessica's process and her struggle. Ashley does not get to pick and choose.

Be careful whose life you envy, and be careful what you ask for and where your heart of jealousy lies, because, at the end of the day, you too are going through a process. Are you so busy wanting another person's blessings that you can't see that God called you to be a diamond so you do not need to be reaching for copper?

I know it's hard to look at other people's dreams come true and try to rejoice for them when you are in your process, but the thing is you do not know their story. You do not know what it took for them to get to their promise. *We all face trials*, we all face storms, and just because the people around you are getting blessed does not mean that God forgot you. It means they finished their part of their process for that particular promise, and now that process is done, they will go through another process. They trusted God and let it go. They believed God for the impossible, and they allowed God before them. It is important in life that you do not blame God for your circumstance, but that you humble yourself under the hand of the Almighty God and allow His control over your life.

Be careful whose life you envy.

Trust me, I get what it is like to look at other people and want what they have and want to be where they are. When Brandon and I were dating, my sister got married and the people around me were getting engaged, and I wanted that. I wanted Brandon to just hurry up and propose already— even though I knew it was not the right time, and we were still growing. I had to walk through my storm, not my sister's, not my friends', but my storm. Brandon and I, whenever we felt weak, broken, or felt an urgency to jump ahead of the process, we would remind each other we were respecting the process, and, oh boy, did I say it was hard? (LOL.)

We wanted to just run headfirst into what we believed was right for us, but God wanted to mature us and complete us before we could get married. We had to respect the process. If we had jumped in our timing instead of God's timing, then we would have missed out on the process, and if we missed the process then we would not have gained perseverance, and without perseverance we would not have been able to make it to completion. We had to trust God's hand over us and not allow anything around us to detour us from God's path for our lives.

So now I ask you: What would happen if you stopped right now and said, "I am over the process and I am done with this"? Could you be ruining your wholeness in Christ because of your lack of respect to walk with Him through the process?

Listen, I don't want you to give up. What am I saying? You *cannot* give up. I will not allow you to! Do not lose hope, and do not become envious of the people around you getting blessed. You have to understand that your story is unique and God is creating a best seller for Himself out of your trials and circumstances.

I am speaking to the broken, scared, hurting, and lost *you*. God has not forgotten about you, and He will do what He said. I know you are rejoicing for the people around you and still wondering when your turn will be. I want to tell you that it is through fire, shattering, and processing that God molds a beautiful diamond. And a diamond is well worth the wait.

Let me pause here to say that I am honored that you are allowing me to be a help to you. Will you let me pray for you now?

I pray that you have faith that is bigger than a mustard seed. I pray that you desire faith that is bigger than that. I pray that your faith is to speak for, to fight for, and to push for. I pray that you understand that the power of your faith can produce

God has not forgotten about you, and He will do what He said.

your purpose. I pray that you understand that this is the beginning of something bigger than you can even fathom. I pray that you become a supernatural thinker because God can do exceedingly and abundantly above anything you could ask or think, so I pray that you begin to think supernaturally so that He can do above that. I pray that you think big, believe big, and that you know big and supersede big. I pray that you understand that this faithing it thing is not just a thing but it is an ethical term that you will begin to live by that you will faith fight to your purpose. I pray that you understand that the enemy is after your faith because he understands the power behind it. I pray that you take a hold of your faith and use it to benefit you, not shake you. I pray that you become a faither. Amen.

Scan this code for Cora's Chapter 2
PRAYER FOR YOU!

Or Visit
WWW.CORAJAKESCOLEMAN.COM

THREE

Fighting Faith

Because of your unbelief; for assuredly, I say to you,
if you have faith as a mustard seed, you will say to
this mountain, "Move from here to there" and it will
move; and nothing will be impossible for you.

(MATTHEW 17:20)

"Process" has a sister, and her name is "Faith." When I am in a stage of process and I am fighting with my faith, I call that "faithing it." And here's the good news—as long as you fight with your faith there is nothing you can't do!

It is through faith that your promise is possible.

It is through faith that your purpose is fulfilled.

And it is through faith that your process finally comes to a victorious end!

Faith defines your level of outcome. If your faith is big, your blessing is big. We can see this by going back to Job. Job had big faith and so, after his process and his struggle, he had a big blessing.

As long as you fight with your faith, there is nothing you can't do!

Some of us do not have enough faith so we are not moving toward a big outcome. That's why Jesus stressed, "Because of your unbelief; for assuredly I say to you, if you have faith as a mustard seed, you will say to this mountain, 'Move from here to there' and it will move; and nothing will be impossible for you" (Matthew 17:20).

What Are You Believing In?

I wonder—what level of faith do you have? What level of faith do I have? Does our faith match up with the blessing for which we are asking of God? Does our faith match up with the promise God told us we'd receive? The problem is that we are asking for big blessings, and we have so little faith that we aren't seeing results.

Without faith in our process we are not going to make it. To begin with, we know that the biblical definition of faith is this:

Faith is the substance of things hoped for, the evidence of things not seen (Hebrews 11:1).

The breakdown of that statement? You must believe in your promise and know it is coming even if you do not see it.

Can you believe without fight? Can you have faith without fight? I say no.

Merriam-Webster's defines *faith* as a strong "belief in something or someone." Some of us choose to have more faith in things we *can* see instead of what we cannot see. Faith is a strong belief in something.

Now, let's think about you and your process. What are you believing in? What are you trusting God for in your life? Is the enemy defining your faith or are you defining your faith? Sometimes we can become so interested in the blessings that we *can* see, that we have no faith in God's ability to do the things we cannot see.

The other half of *Webster's* definition of faith is a strong belief in someone—"a person." Some of us have trusted people to give us something instead of trusting the God who is preparing a place for us. It is time for us to start putting our strength in God instead of our logic, our thoughts, and our opinions.

Can you believe without fight?

Jesus' statement about faith in Matthew 17:20 came because the disciples did not have faith in their ability.

Here's the story from Matthew 17. A man with a demon-possessed son came to Jesus for help. What is so amazing about the story is that the father says, "I went to the disciples and they could not heal him." Now, Jesus spoke to the demon and it was removed. The disciples were shocked, and they wanted to know why it did not work for them. That's when Jesus responded, "Because of your unbelief; for assuredly, I say to you, if you have faith as a mustard seed, you can say to this mountain, 'Move from here to there' and it will move; and nothing will be impossible for you "(Matthew 17:20).

Don't Wait to See Before You Believe

They did not have faith in themselves. They did not have that fight within themselves to cast the demon out. Without belief in your power through Jesus, you have no power. Jesus is calling for a believing generation, a faith-fighting generation!

We can get so caught up in what we can *see* that God cannot use us.

We can get so consumed by doubt in our own ability that God cannot use us.

We can get so lazy in our belief in God that He cannot use us.

We need to get our power back!

Too often we wait to see it before we can believe it, and we don't match our day-to-day lives with our faith in God. Do you have faith enough to believe what God said and move on it, even if He does not give you a sign? In the days before creation, God was just God. He did not have to give any signs, numbers, or a divine message through a prophet. He was just God. We (myself included) have gotten caught up in the "God, show me a sign" prayer. Really, all that means is, "God, I do not really believe that I heard You, and I need You to confirm Your voice because I have strayed so far away from You that I do not know for sure if that is You." Have you strayed so far away from God that you are not confident that you can hear His voice? I understand. I was there.

It's possible that you are still in the same process stage and going through the same test over and over again because you have disconnected from God's voice, and He is simply testing your faith. We repeat prayers over and over again as if God did not hear us the first time. Yet Jesus told us if we have just a little faith we can move a mountain. He did not say we would have to repeat over and over again to the mountain before it moved. Speak one time with just a little faith. Jesus did not repeat to the boy over and over again to be healed. He spoke one time, and it was so.

So my question to you is, have you gotten so broken that you cannot believe? Have you gotten so cut that you do not believe in your ability or your relationship with God? Are you choosing to allow your circumstance to detour you from the plan God has set before you? Have you forgotten God's voice? Are you praying for signs and wonders because you have lost your faith? Are you so lost in your process that you forgot you are a child of God?

Faith for the "Now Generation"

There was a time when I wondered, why did Jesus say we can move a mountain and not a rock or a pebble? And why did He not say, "If you have faith like a mountain you can move a mountain?"

Then I began to evaluate myself and us as a people. I came to the conclusion that those words from Jesus are prophetic for the "now generation." One time Jesus even said, "You are an unbelieving and perverse generation." Even people who were alive in Jesus' day were losing faith and belief in themselves. If you lose faith and belief in yourself, then you lose faith and belief in God. He knew that we were going to start losing our faith, and He knew we would have mountains, and in a plea for us to believe that He can do it *all*, He said, "If you can just have faith the size of a mustard seed, you can move your mountain." He asked for something small. He stressed that if you had that small thing you could move that big thing. A mustard seed is about 3 mm in size. Jesus was pleading with us, "If you just believe this small, I can do something so big!"

The sad part is that we use this Scripture as our "go-to prayer" when we are at our breaking point. Then we say, "Lord, You said if I have faith the size of a mustard seed, I can move mountains. Please, Lord, move this mountain!" At that point we're thinking, *Surely I have more faith than the size of a mustard seed!* Unfortunately, we do not, and that is why we end up staying tossed around in our storm.

You cannot ask God to decrease your struggle until you ask Him to increase your faith.

You cannot ask God to decrease your struggle until you ask Him to increase your faith. When we pray for our dreams and they do not happen right away, we can allow our circumstances to chip away at our faith in God. Or we can choose to allow the cutting to shape us and yield to the skillful hands of the Master Carpenter, Jesus Christ.

So this chapter is a match that I am placing in you. I want you to know I understand that in the middle of a broken place it is hard to believe God.

With God you can achieve the unthinkable, and with God you can conceive the impossible. The biggest part of this struggle is faith.

We can tell our thoughts to "faith it"! To faith your logic (meaning your thoughts, your opinions, and your perspective of life) is to announce to your logic, "God is seeing me through this because I can't see for myself."

I recently made a decision to faith my logic to trust God in all that I do and that whatever happened was all in God's hands. I prepared myself for this choice by writing to God the things that I wanted specifically. I prayed to God once for what I needed and I stood back and praised Him for it in advance.

Why don't you do that too? You can write down what you are seeking, and begin to believe God like never before—even if you are writing for God to help you believe. You cannot remove yourself from a stagnant place without first realizing that you have placed yourself there by not believing in God, and not believing in yourself, and not fighting your storm with faith. You have to want to be better in order to get to better. You have to want to leap in order to get to the top. If you can start faithing it (fighting with faith) then you have the ability to conquer this.

Jesus Ministered from the Cross

Consider Jesus. Jesus was broken, bruised, and beaten, and we believed in Him. And it was in His breaking that He became a King. He was a carpenter in the process of greatness, and it was after His beating, after His bruises, after they nailed His bleeding body on the cross, and He rose again, that He became a King.

My friend, God is breaking you into your crown. I want you to understand that without believing what He said and fighting, you cannot get to the other side. God used His crucifixion to *be* a ministry. And here you are, waiting to be healed and come out whole before you minister from your own cross. When Jesus ministered to the people and hung from the cross, He went through His process in the face of His people.

Post Up!

It's time to get your faith back! It's time for you to face yourself and ask God to reignite in you the passion for Him so that you can fight the enemy. It's time for you to realize that you were built in the image of a man who was broken for us. Theologians will be quick to interject that Jesus did not endure physically broken bones, but Jesus said at Passover, "Take eat. This is my body which was broken for you!" (see Matthew 26:26). So I am saying His body and His emotions and His spirit were cut, broken, and shaped into perfection when He obeyed God and went to the cross.

Where is *your* fight? Where is *your* faith?

You are standing in the middle of your storm, saying, "I trust You, God," but do you?

Do not allow the beating of your process to take away your faith. You need to fight back. The enemy cannot take what you do not put in his face. My daughter watches *Dora the Explorer* animated TV series, and one of my favorite things is when Swiper (the enemy) shows up and he wants to take something from Dora, and they have to say, "Swiper, no swiping," and sometimes he goes away, but sometimes he takes something, and they say, "Aw, man!" But they immediately start searching for what he took, and try to put it back in its rightful place. We can learn something from Dora here. Do you just say, "Aw, man!" and walk away? Or do you fight back and begin to search in your spirit.

Allow God to stir up the fight in you. It's time for you to begin faithing it. Things are going to happen to you, and you are going to get hurt, but we have already learned that is your process, and now we know that we have to match our faith with our process. Stop praying for mustard seed faith. Ask God to give you faith the size of a mountain. What would happen if you faced your trial with mountain-sized faith? A mountain-sized fight!

My daughter is in kindergarten, and a little boy was bullying her. Almost every day she would come home with an incident report that he scratched her, hit her, or did something just crazy. My husband sat her down, and began to show her how to protect herself and post up.

We told her, "There will be all types of enemies in your life, and when they approach you and they try to hurt you, then you have to protect yourself. You have to fight back."

Next time she went to school and he tried to scratch her, all she did was post up, and he backed down.

What would happen if you were in the middle of a whirlwind, and you just posted up with faith? Is your faith strong enough to stop your storm? Is your faith strong enough to stand up for itself?

You may be believing God for a relationship, a healing, a house, job, car, or anything. Whatever it is you believe God for you must understand that it is through your faithing that you get it. And if mustard seed faith can move one mountain, imagine what mountain-sized faith could move. It's time for faithing. It's time for real faith! God is calling His children. You must hear His voice and know it's Him and move by His perfect will. It is in your sincere trust and belief in God that you can be saved from the dangers that the enemy brings. Sometimes that danger is real.

My Struggle, My Story

Did you read the story about my accident in the introduction?

I was in the worst accident of my life. Although I came out of it without a scratch or a bruise, I found out the next day during a CAT scan that I had a 7 cm cyst on one ovary and a 9 cm cyst on my other ovary. In short, that one car accident led to me discovering two cysts, the loss of an ovary, the loss of a fallopian tube, and a news flash from the doctor that it wasn't probable for me to get pregnant without going through in vitro fertilization (IVF).

God gave me a wonderful husband that had enough faith to fight for the both of us. We went through the IVF cycle, and it didn't work out. That was another pain, and I asked, "God, why me?" But that led us to adopt our beautiful daughter, Amauri. We rested and went through another IVF cycle. I went through the acupuncture, the pineapples, and the legs up, and all the tricks, and we found out it didn't work this time either.

A few months after going through the pain of the failed fertilizations, my godsister Michelle called me. She wanted me to go with her into the birthing room, and I did. I witnessed the birth of my godson, and I was honored to cut the umbilical cord. Since that day, I have been gifted to raise him. He is an amazing gift, one I wouldn't have even accepted if I was pregnant.

Why am I telling you all of this? I am telling you this because I want you to know that no matter what you're going through, you can overcome and be victorious. I could have spent my time crying over the loss of my ovary and fallopian tube, or I could thank God because I am still able to overcome and win and be victorious.

Not Bound by Brokenness

Don't spend any more time asking God, "Why me?" You have been considered for the struggle because there is something great to be produced through you. You have been considered for the struggle because God is about to make you a survivor and a successor of your storm. Don't focus on the broken, focus on the blessing. You don't need to worry about the pains of process and the *why me?* Really, you must ask yourself, "Why not me?" For every broken piece God is planting a blessing. You are not being broken for no reason, you are being broken on purpose. You are going through the pains because God is about to birth something beautiful through you.

You are not bound by your brokenness, you are lifted from it. I could still be looking at the car accident, but I stepped into the purpose of the pain. Stop searching for the why me, and start searching for the blessing. If you don't, you will miss out on what God has and where you are meant to go because you have stopped yourself from soaring. It's time to soar, sweetheart, soar. God chose you because you are called to be of great power.

Don't focus on the broken, focus on the blessing.

Your struggle is because you have a purpose.

Your struggle is because you are powerful.

Your struggle is because you have a message.

When you can understand that you aren't the average person, then you will know that your purpose is powerful. Your pain is powerful. You are a Kingdom kid, so you will have to go through some things, but catch what I am saying: You will go *through* them, and by faithing it, you will get to the other side!

You are covered by the blood of the Lamb. If God is living in you, then you have a hedge of protection camped around you, and whatever storm the enemy brings you must rear up like Job and know that your God is greater, bigger, and stronger than anything you could be facing. Your time to believe God is now.

You are whole when your fight matches with your belief. The woman with the issue of blood bled for twelve years. She was hurting, but as soon as she heard Jesus was near she got out of her bed, and she took her fight and her faith to Jesus. She crawled and climbed through the crowd and moved while bleeding to get her healing. She did not care about the people or the crowd! Her faith and her fight was to press in far enough—she just wanted a piece of Jesus' clothing to touch. She believed after bleeding for twelve years, "If I can just get to His hem I can be healed."

How many of you can believe God like that after twelve years of being broken and hurt? You can put your shoes on and drape yourself and climb through a crowd to get to your promise. And if you remember, when she climbed through the crowd and she touched His hem, Jesus immediately knew He had been touched. When He turned around and saw her, He pulled her up and He said, "Go, for your faith has made you *whole*" (see Mark 5:34). That goes back to our first chapter: God is pulling you up through a process so that you can be whole.

I want to speak to the tired you. You have been hurt time and time again. Things have been taken from you after you pled with God to hold on to them, and now you do not believe God cares for you. You do not believe God hears you. I want to tell you that He hears you, and He is there with you, and He's holding you, but it is your faith that He is after. If you will trust God, you can get to His hem.

You cannot pray to a God you do not believe in.

You cannot pray to a God you have lost faith in.

You cannot pray to a God you do not even have mustard seed faith for.

Get Real with God

My faith has been shaken at times, but my heart for God wasn't. I understand that as a child of the King, I must go through things that will shake me. I understand that just as any relationship sometimes I will get upset with Him, I will get sad with Him, I will get hurt with Him, but I will also get happy with Him, overcome with Him, reach milestones with Him, fall more in love with Him. The point is, I will be with Him! I am in a relationship with Christ so that although He slay me, shake me, and crush me, I will trust that at the end of it all I will receive a crown.

You have to be real with God. He knows your every thought. He knows you are mad when it does not work out the way you wanted it to. He knows that you are breaking apart on the inside. He knows you are confused, He knows you really wanted it, but I want you to start trusting Him for the expected end of your trials.

I know. You are probably saying, "Cora, how?" You are being cut to be beautiful, and God is not saying no because He does not love you. He is saying no because it is not time, and that if you draw unto Him then He will draw into you. It's easy to get a no and find your faith shaken, but that's why I am calling it a challenge. Because no matter how hard you get cut, no matter how bad it is, you have to look and say, "Though You slay me, no matter how hurt and heart-broken I am, I will trust You."

That is how you do it. Trust Him in your brokenness. Trust Him in your heartbreak. You trust Him in your anger, and you tell Him. You share with God your truth. When I had to go through heart-break, I had to go before the Lord with my truth, saying, "God, I really wanted that! I am sad, angry, hurt, and heartbroken that you did not give me what my heart desired. I feel like You don't care about my desire, my hope, or my vision."

Part of having faith in God is believing in Him when things don't make sense—believing God when things don't work out.

The enemy's motive is to destroy your faith in God, because if the enemy can take your faith then he can take your fight. You are empowered by God when you choose Him above the pain you are going through. You need to believe God can and will be greater than your storm. A storm walked through alone is a storm that cannot end and will not have peace, but when you walk through your storm with God then you have peace and power. You will have the access to get through it because of who you have decided to work with.

A Choice to Make

As we end this chapter together, I want to challenge you today to make a choice. I challenge you to stand in the face of negativity and say, "I rebuke you, devil, for making me not believe God for what He said. And today I am faithing my logic, my thoughts, and my perceptions."

Obstacles will come—face them with faith. More importantly, face them with God.

Give God all of you. Stop hiding from God and begin to reveal yourself. Remember, He knows all and sees all. Be willing to be submissive and open to giving Him the embarrassing things. Open your heart to God—the broken pieces, the hard and hollow pieces, and open it up to God. You can be great, just strengthen your faith.

When you fight with faith you are fighting for purpose.

I'm talking to you—yes, you! Don't let your storms shake your faith so much so that you have been shaken out of the ring. It's time for you to get your faith back—claim your power back. You deserve the ability to win. In fact, you have earned the right to win. You are stronger than you think, and this shaking was supposed to stop you but no more.

You won't be hindered by the storm. You will use the storm to catapult you into your destiny. God needs you to overtake the Kingdom.

You are reading this page in this book because God wants you and me to talk about this right now. I want you to know that God isn't against you—He wants you to win! The bad stuff happened, and you

You are empowered by God when you choose Him above the pain you are going through.

were hurt but you aren't dead. You still have life. You still have fight! So it's time! We are not to sit down in our hurt, sadness, anger, and brokenness anymore. We are fighting with faith. Today, starting right now, this moment, we are faithing it!

I have such an earnest desire to see you cross over into your promise! Please, let me pray with you!

I pray that God strengthens your faith in this season and that you open up to Him. I pray you are vulnerable to God. I pray that God refreshes your relationship with Him and shows you that He is for you. I pray that God lifts you up before great men, and that He walks you through the steps that are needed in order for you to pursue your purpose. I pray that you begin to resist the devil and confront the enemy that is within. I pray that your strongholds be broken and that the yoke that has you bound and that has made you stop trusting and stop having faith in God, I pray that it be loosed right now in the name of Jesus. I pray that this moment right now you are ignited in purpose and that you begin to develop a real relationship with Christ. You are great! I pray you begin to walk in that. In the name of Jesus, it is so. And so it is. Amen.

Scan this code for Cora's Chapter 3
PRAYER FOR YOU!

Or Visit
WWW.CORAJAKESCOLEMAN.COM

FOUR

The YES in the Burning Bush

The Lord your God, who goes before you,
He will fight for you, according to all He
did for you in Egypt before your eyes.

(DEUTERONOMY 1:30, AND ALL OF CHAPTER ONE!)

One of our needs as human beings is to know who is with us. Who believes in me? Who's got my back if things go wrong? It's possible to become so caught up in ourselves that we cannot see that God is our back support. Let me share a story from the Bible that I hope will encourage your heart, because I want you to know that you are not alone.

I want to bring you to a moment in the life of Moses. Moses was tending to the flock as normal when in the distance he saw a bush. The bush was on fire, but it was not burning down to the ground. He decided to go toward this bush to see this strange sight. When he got there, the Bible says that God called for him from within the bush, and Moses answered, "Here I am" (see Exodus 3). Now you must understand, that is the step that so many of us are missing. God calls for us to invite us into His purpose, but because we are so astray from His voice we do not answer. When God announced Himself, Moses hid his face because he did not want to look at God.

God is our back support.

Moses was told to go and save the Israelites because God had heard their cries. So many of us are crying out to God, and we do not even realize that He has come or that He is sending someone on our behalf to save us. The beautiful part of this is that Moses in his humility questioned God: "Who am I to go to them and demand this?" And the response from the Lord is what brings me to back support. God said to him, "Go, and I will be with you." I want you to realize that it is not about you—it is about who is with you. God was Moses' back support as he traveled back to Egypt to get the Israelites to the promise. God told Moses, "I have your back. I am with you."

This is the big YES in the burning bush! God says, "YES, it is time for Me to send you into your destiny, the purpose for which I made you." Moses has questions, but ultimately he says, "YES, I will do all that You say." There was a yes to purpose and a yes to going. And when God says yes, He gives a promise to go behind Moses and be his back support. If God says yes to you and others don't, it doesn't matter, as long as you say yes in response to God!

So when the Israelites started acting funny and trying to rebel, Moses was like, "Wait a minute, did you not see that God went before us and fought for us, and got us out of our storm? Did you not see that God was with us?" Moses was angry then, and we need to watch that we don't become the same people he was angry with!

The Trap of Vulnerability

After the people complained in his ear, Moses was discouraged and he was vulnerable. So Moses and Aaron left the presence of the people and went together to the door of the tabernacle. The glory of God Almighty appeared to them there! God told Moses and Aaron to take the rod with them and go to a large rock in the wilderness. But instead of striking the rock with the long staff, God told Moses to speak to the rock. Now, speaking to a rock is strange but, remember, I told you that you can't be afraid of strange things if you're going to get to your destiny with God.

Moses and Aaron got all the people to gather around the big rock, but by that time Moses was so frustrated with the people he said, "Hear now, you rebels!" (See Numbers 20.)

Moses was told to speak to the rock, but the sin of the people made him so angry that he struck the rock instead. In short, this emotional outburst caused Moses to disobey God. Because of his vulnerability, he was easily manipulated into emotional outbursts and unchecked anger, and he missed out on leading the people into the Promised Land. You will miss out on your promise when you remain vulnerable to the wrong thing. When you become vulnerable to anger, then it consumes you. You can be sure that the enemy works very well with anger. When you become vulnerable to bitterness, it consumes you and the enemy works well with bitterness.

Whatever you are vulnerable to will consume you. I want you to become vulnerable to God so that He can consume you. You are stronger than you know! When we don't understand how God could allow certain things to happen to us, we can start to push away from God. Don't do it! The more you push away from God, the longer you leave the door open for negative spirits to enter. Stop giving the enemy access to doors he should've never had the key to. Don't make yourself vulnerable!

Worship while you wait for victory.

When we read the full text in the first chapter of Deuteronomy, we find that the people were in rebellion. They were so close to the Promised Land, the land flowing with milk and honey. God had blessed them and wanted to bless them again. Moses told them to go in, but even though they trusted Moses before, they did not trust him this time.

Become vulnerable to God so that He can consume you.

They said, "Well, send someone up there before us to see if it's okay." Instead of saying, "God said go, and it is well," Moses said that the people had a good idea, so he does it. The people were manipulating Moses' faith.

The people were untrusting. They sent people up to look over the Promised Land to see if the land was good, and even after hearing it was good they still rebelled against God. They allowed their surroundings to put fear in them. The people were taller and the walls were bigger, and they allowed that to keep them from moving forward. Because of their lack of trust and unbelief, they even went as far as to say the Lord hated them!

That's when Moses stepped in and told the people, "The Lord your God, who is going before you, will fight for you, as He did for you in Egypt, before your very eyes" (Deuteronomy 1:30 NIV). He reminds them how God showed up for them in Egypt, how He carried them from their struggle to safety, and even in the midst of all of that they still did not trust God, and they continued to rebel against God.

Moses is really just letting them have it! They did not allow God to be their back support and show them the way. Because of their inability to trust God, even after they had trusted God all this time, they were forbidden access to the Promised Land. How many of us are allowing our fear of what we see keep us from believing God?

Moses walked into Egypt and with God's power delivered them from their struggle, their process, and led them over the sea. Moses got them to safety and showed God's miraculous works, and they still rebelled against the Lord. Moses had believed in God all this time, but after so many years he allowed himself to be wavered and manipulated. So because he allowed the people to shake him, he was forbidden from the Promised Land as well. He tells them basically that Caleb and Joshua are the only ones who followed the Lord, and they are the only ones, along with the children under twenty-one years of age, who will be able to inherit the Promised Land. When we choose not to trust God, we choose to lose our inheritance.

A big part of allowing God to be your support is allowing God to lead you. That means God is both behind you and before you. The people Moses allowed to challenge his faith and his ability to hear from God kept him from the Promised Land. The leadership to the Promised Land was given to Joshua. Sometimes we allow the people around us to change our thoughts and waver our faith, and we miss out on our blessing because we slipped on our faith.

After Moses read the people their rights, then they wanted to fight, but by then it was too late. God said, "Do not go up and fight, because I will not be with you. You will be defeated by your enemies" (Deuteronomy 1:42 NIV). You cannot wait until your promise is taken to believe God. You have to believe God in the ups and the downs, no matter what it looks like. The minute you lose God's support, the minute He isn't with you, then your enemies will defeat you.

They did not know that God was their back support, and Moses was being used to guide them through as God instructed him. He was trying to get the people to understand the God of hope, support, and fight he encountered at the bush. He reminded them, "God went before us and fought for our people." He tried to get the people to see the God he had trusted all this time. They would not believe.

What Kicks Us Away from Our Promise

What kicks us away from our promise? Could it be that we can talk about the storms God took us through, but we cannot trust God in the storm we are standing in?

What kicks us away from healing the broken? Could it be that we believe that we have to be perfect in order to be used?

God chose Moses from a burning place. Even though Moses stuttered and had low self-esteem, God chose him and God believed in him.

The beautiful part is that God chose him from birth, for just as he was drawn out of the water he would draw His people out! And it was because of Moses' heart toward God that he was able to be used. He was not a prince anymore, he was just Moses and he was used by God to move all of the Israelites to freedom.

In the end, when God talked to Moses from the burning bush, He was telling Moses, "Yes, I believe in you." Ultimately, Moses said yes to God. Equally important, Moses took that one "I believe in you" from God to leap into his destiny. I want you to understand that your destiny is tied to the yes in the burning bush. It is not about where you are standing, it is about where your heart is and what you are walking toward. God knew your purpose from the beginning of time, and He knew that you would have an encounter with a burning bush of your own, and that you would have to choose to either walk with God or wait for the people around you to make your choice for you. You cannot allow the people around you to define where God chooses for you to go.

What would have happened if Moses had said, "I can't," and walked away?

What would have happened if Moses had waited for his friends to say, "Yes, Moses! You can do it!"?

What would have happened if Moses had waited for the world's yes instead of walking on God's yes?

Your destiny is tied to the yes in the burning bush.

We can wait for the world to gratify us, and in that waiting we have missed that God already said yes. This is a good place to check ourselves. Have we been so consumed by getting our friends to support our dream that we have missed our encounter with God's yes? We can lose what was meant for us while waiting around for the world to support us.

Walking toward the Strange Thing

Moses was tending the flock when he saw a strange thing. How many of us are missing God because of our inability to walk toward the strange things? How many of us are waiting for someone to say, "Oh, yes, you are called to be great," instead of believing what God already said? Is it possible that we are trying to find our place in the world when God has already given us an assignment? What do you do when you have missed God's approval waiting on the world's yes? I need you to realize that the only support you need is the support of God's belief in you, and God's yes. Move in what God said, not what the world said.

I am reminded of Sarah when the angel told her she would conceive and she laughed (see Genesis 18:1–15). Some of us are hearing strange assignments from God, and we are laughing. How long will you laugh at God's promise because you think you are too old or it isn't naturally possible? Sometimes God is bringing forth amazing miracles because of your amazing storm, and if you would understand that God is with you in the midst of the storm then you will be more open to the miracle. We must know, believe, and walk in what God said for us to do and stop waiting for natural responses to a spiritual revelation.

God Is Your Back Support

I want to talk to you about allowing God to be your back support. You cannot wait on the people around you to push you, and truth be told if you are waiting for your friends to give you a yes then you are not dreaming big enough. You need to have a vision and purpose so big for your life that the only person who can make it happen or see it through is God.

Who are you allowing to be your back support?

Who are you allowing to speak into your life?

Who are you allowing to motivate and push you?

When Moses was standing at the burning bush, he was nervous and did not know what to do. God was already preparing a place for him. He was already getting the people prepared for Moses. We need to know that if God gives us an assignment, He is already working on the people ahead of time. I know what you are saying—if God prepared the elders and ministers to listen to Moses, why not Pharaoh? It's because of the need for the process. Moses had to have a challenge in order to get the people to the promise. Even when God knows you are going to win in the end, that does not mean you will not have great challenges.

If you can acknowledge God as your back support, and you can know God is preparing the people for you ahead of time, then you can move forward. So we understand first that God is our back support, but the other wonderful thing about the story is that Moses also had his brother, wife, and sister. Part of what made Moses so powerful is that he had support backing him. He had God, his family, his wife, and his people. You cannot move forward until you have people behind you to push you to your next level. It is in God's power that Moses was able to move miraculously. Moses believed God, and he did everything God told him to do to get the people to the promise.

If you do not have your family to support you, then you move on that one "I believe in you" that you hear from the Lord. You move on that one "you can do this," and you move on the one encounter that you have with your figurative burning bush. Moses had an encounter with God for every new step he had to take. After his first encounter, he became sensitive and vulnerable to the Spirit of God, so much so that he was consumed and visited by the Spirit of God. Why am I saying this? Because Moses took that one go from God, and he matched it with faith. That's how he fulfilled his purpose.

Let God Move You

What would happen if you took that one yes from God? How many people could you get to their promise if you used your one yes from God to move you?

Moses took that one yes and plagues were initiated and lives changed.

Moses took that one yes and the people followed him.

Moses took that one yes and his enemies were behind him.

Moses took that one yes and moved all of God's people into the promise.

All that action started with that one simple yes. When you can go when God says go, you can move through the water and obtain your purpose. My hope is that you do not stand at the burning bush waiting for other people to believe in the yes God gave you, but that you move and carry people to the promise. Walk out your yes to God and He will surely keep His yes promises to you.

You must allow yourself to have the encounter with God so the Spirit can consume you. When people see God's power in you, then they will get behind the God in you. Stop trying to lead yourself to your purpose and promise, and allow God to lead you.

I daresay that you can challenge God to use you in a major capacity according to your storm. I refuse to allow the Lord to let the enemy take me through great tribulation, and me not come out stronger, bigger, better, and more powerful than when I started. My storms must match my impact of ministry. I refuse to allow the enemy to believe that God will not get the glory out of every storm, mountain, and adversity that I face. I am more than a conqueror, and I know that God is with me. Once you understand that you have the ultimate support, then you can do ultimate moves.

My storms must match my impact of ministry.

When I was seven years old, my father sat us all down and said God told him to move to Texas. At the time it was crazy. We had a good life, we were in a nice home, and we knew no one in Texas. All of our friends and family were in West Virginia. None of that mattered. My dad had a burning bush encounter, and God said go, and he moved on it. We were nervous but we understood that if God said yes to Daddy, we were going to go. We supported my dad's burning bush moment, and we moved. When we moved, my dad moved over ten families with him. Just as Moses did, my dad went on God's yes and he pulled families into the promise. My father allowed God to be his back support and, because of that, he was able to pull other people out.

When we moved, doors began to fly open, and it's been the most amazing experience of our lives. When you can trust God, He can move you to your destiny. When you can trust God, He can show you things you know not of. It was then at an early age that I understood if God speaks to you, even in fear, nervousness, and uncertainty, you move no matter what. If you have crazy belief, then God can do crazy things. We had an expectancy of greatness, and God gave us just that.

What are you expecting from God? The win is in your ability to believe that God is supporting you, even in the worst of times.

All great things come through because of support. When you are about to start a diet, you look for an accountability partner. You lose more weight when you have an accountability partner than when you don't, and that is because greatness comes with support. Greatness happens when you have someone cheering on what you think is impossible. Greatness comes when you understand that you cannot do this without help. If God gave you a yes or a go, that means He has your back. That means that He is with you, and He is your back support.

We all fall short of the glory of God, but the power is in your ability to get back up.

The power is in your ability to chase after God.

Our power is in our search for Christ and our understanding that there is beauty in our broken things. Then we can say, "I am strong, and God gave me a yes and I will run with that."

Hear God and Say, "Yes"

Say yes to the process, yes to the test and trials. Later on, we can look at our trials as treasures and then we can win in the end. You will go through ups and downs, but stand on the yes that God gave you. Some of us have moved because we thought it was God speaking, and we are now realizing it wasn't Him. You know who you are in Christ, and once you do that you can redevelop your relationship with Christ, and once you do that then you can hear from Christ.

Some of us have to admit we have strayed, and our prayer life needs to be: "Lord, help me to redevelop my commitment with You. Help me to run back to You. Help me to hear You, and do not allow me to walk toward my will, but only Yours."

If you text friends, Facebook friends, or tweet friends more than you talk to God, then you cannot hear Him. You have to be so close to God that there is no doubt in His instructions to you. You have to be so close to God that the people around you see God in you. That does not mean you should go around quoting Scriptures every hour and become overwhelmingly spiritual. That means that you show your pure heart toward Christ. You are not always going to get it right, and there are going to be times that you fall, but when God is your back support you can do anything.

Some of us have placed people where we need to place God.

Some of us have placed people's opinions of us where God's thoughts of us need to be. Some of us must step away from our own will and step into God's true desire and hope.

The people rebelled against God and began to worship calves, commit adultery, murder, and just jump into the world. After all God did for them, they left His presence. They left behind His instruction and they rebelled. We cannot become the people of the world—we must become the changers of the world. We cannot begin to break the rules God placed and pray for the blessings of God. We must be renewed from the inside out, and allow God to be with us. What made Moses powerful was not the bush or the staff or the plagues. What made Moses powerful is that God said, "Go, and I will be with you." Some of us have gone without God being with us, and then we wonder why miracles are not happening. We have to understand that it was the God with Moses who made him powerful.

We cannot become the people of the world—we must become the changers of the world.

With God, I Can Do This

Your power is in God, not in people. Your power is in your walk in Christ, not in your actions in the world. When Moses said yes to God, God did not once bring up where Moses came from. In fact, He used new things to show His support of Moses. Do not limit God's ability by staying in what you went through during your process. It is your walk toward Christ that makes you great, not the steps you took without Him.

The Bible says, "With God *all things are possible*" (Matthew 19:26 NIV). It's a simple Scripture, and we hear it often, but we must live by this Scripture.

I cannot be great without God—it's not possible.

My marriage cannot succeed without God—it's not possible.

My job cannot succeed without God—it's not possible.

I will not get that raise without God—it's not possible.

My child won't survive cancer without God—it's not possible.

My parenting won't be a success without God—it's not possible.

You must be consumed by God, supported by God, and standing with God because with God *all* things are possible! With God I can do this!

Let God fight your battle. Let Him in. Let Him bring forth your success through your submission to Him. God is a better fighter, better provider, better leader, and just better all around than we are. You will win when you remove your hands off of God's plans for your life and let Him orchestrate it.

Moses looked at the people, and he pleaded with them, "Wait! God fought for us. We got here because of God."

Wait! You cannot become great without back support. Your hope, your legacy, and your promise are in the God who supports you.

I am eager to pray over you right now!

I pray that God will be your first choice of support. I pray that you begin to see yourself through the eyes of God. I pray that you would begin to walk in your destiny without pain and hurt weighing you down. I pray that you would remove your hands and begin to fight with your faith. I pray that God grant you the desire and discipline to be able to obtain what He has for you. I pray that you are able to stand before your mountains and command them to move, and they be moved. I pray that you stand up for your purpose and you gain your power. I pray that you begin to live life and make every decision count. You will come out of this by the power of the Holy Ghost, and I thank God that you are free to be with God, and, being with Him, you are free and it is so and so it is by the power of the Holy Ghost. Amen.

Let's continue this journey of faithing it together…

Scan this code for Cora's Chapter 4
PRAYER FOR YOU!

Or Visit
WWW.CORAJAKESCOLEMAN.COM

FIVE

Delights, Desires, and Dysfunctions

*Delight yourself also in the Lord, and
He shall give you the desires of your heart.*

(Psalm 37:4)

I f I could invite you into my home right now at the beginning of this chapter and sit down with you over coffee, I would ask you this question: What truly delights your soul? I mean, what thought can make you smile even when nobody is in the room?

For me, I'd have to say that nothing delights my soul in this life as much as welcoming a new baby into the family. It doesn't matter if that baby is my child or my niece or nephew, there is a delight that stirs the waters in the Jakes and Coleman families whenever a new life is given to us to nurture. That new little one is ours, but a stranger, really. We don't know yet if this baby will play football or play the piano. We don't yet know this little one's favorite color, and we certainly don't know everything this baby's future will hold! We all realize that in the days and years ahead, this precious child will consume much of our time, talents, and treasures. We will spend our time and treasure in what delights us. Jesus said, "Where your treasure is, there your heart will be also" (Matthew 6:21). So where we spend our extra money—that is, the money outside the cost of living—is a pretty good indication of what delights our heart.

But money is no object when it comes to caring for a new son or daughter. We know that it will take time and patience to get to really know this baby. We realize that there will be midnight feedings and rocking chair prayers in the weeks and months to come. Sacrifices will be made to ensure that our baby receives every natural and spiritual blessing that we can give. Yes, it will take a lot of work and sacrifice, but that is nothing compared to the sheer joy of getting to know this new little person and developing a special relationship together.

We will spend our time and treasure in what delights us.

Do you know God feels the same way? When we are born again, He longs to spend His time, talents, and treasure on this newborn child of God. His love for us just increases day by day.

Of course, a newborn doesn't stay tiny forever. That baby will walk, talk, clap, and eventually eat solid food. For a few years, the mother and father are the central joy of that child's life. We all know what happens in adolescence—separation. It's at that point that a child rightly desires separation from his or her parents in order to establish personal identity. I can't say I look forward to the separation part, but it's all a normal stage of growth.

The Spirit of Adoption

It is at this stage of adolescent growth that a child decides whether or not to adopt the parent! Seriously! We know God is good and we may even call Him "Father," but have we allowed that spirit of adoption to flood our souls until nothing and no one delights us like Father God? Maybe we don't need Him in the same way we did when we were first born again, but we still need Him! And He needs us! He wants us! God says to us, "Delight yourself in Me, and I'll give you the desires of your heart."

No one knows us like Father God. No one.

Sometimes we abandon our destiny because we wander off looking for other amusements and delights. God's purpose and dream may fade into the background as we pursue other interests. If that's you, ask God right now to restore you back to His dream and His purpose for your life.

If you do not identify your promise, purpose, or dream, then you don't know what you are fighting for. Do you delight in the Lord? Is your time with God the highlight of your day?

There is so much power and purpose generated when we set aside time alone to delight in God. Of course, we have to stop communicating horizontally via Twitter, Messenger, Snapchat, Facebook, texts, and e-mails, but if we will lay all that aside and listen, God wants to say something to us!

We often get stuck in the part of the Scripture that says God will grant us the desires of our hearts, not understanding that it first said that we must delight ourselves in Him in order for those desires to be granted. So the question then is, how do you know what you want to do? He grants you the desires of your heart according to how much of your heart you have given to Him.

How do you know what your purpose is? This is not a question that comes with an easy answer. But I have found that what the enemy tries to block you from the most is the thing that you are supposed to be going after. In reality, the enemy isn't fighting you for your purpose; he is fighting you for your power. He will try to distract you with any number of things to keep you from pressing and delighting yourself in God because he knows that's where you get your power. The enemy knows that if you head toward delighting yourself in God, then God will open the doors to grant you all your desires. And it stands to reason that when you have the desires of your heart and you are able to see the power of God, then you become more compatible with God, which makes you a force to be reckoned with!

God wants to say something to us!

If you've spent time with God, then He's already put some of those desires within you. You have that passion deep inside somewhere, but the enemy keeps presenting you with distractions to keep you from the very thing that you should go after. The enemy tried to block my fertility, and that is because I delighted myself in God to fight for my promise. With God on my side, I began faithing for my power. Satan is trying to stop me from being a mother. He is trying to stop your progress and your pressing in to delight in God. What is your desire? Delight yourself in God, and you will be able to produce your desire. This is all part of faithing it.

One of our God-given purposes on this earth is to be fruitful and multiply. It's easy to say that this purpose pertains just to women and men being able to have children, but I challenge you to think bigger! God wants you to be fruitful in all things and to multiply in all that you produce. It's important that you know that the very reason you have a desire to do what you want to do is because God placed that desire in you. If God was good enough to place the desire in you, then He should be good enough for you to walk toward and to link up with. If God is for you, then nothing can be against you.

In my personal life, adoption became a focal point of my communication with God. I was diagnosed with infertility even after telling God my entire life that all I wanted was to be a mommy. I could've given up, but instead I decided to get under God's umbrella. When I delighted my life, my marriage, my home, and everything in God, He granted me the desires of my heart by giving me a beautiful daughter. What a joy it is to my heart when she calls me "Mom."

What you must realize is that just because you delight yourself in God doesn't mean that you won't face opposition. You may endure ridicule, backlash, haters, and unwanted and unmerited opinion. If God gives you a yes, just keep pushing and don't give up! I don't care what your desire or what your dream is, when you delight in God and your relationship with Him, then nothing can stop you! In fact, blessings will overtake you, the light will shine on you, and all will work out according to God's perfect will.

Dysfunction, Distraction, and Detours

Now let's talk about the real issue here, and that is dysfunction, distraction, and detours that prevent you from getting to God. If you don't delight yourself in God, how can He can grant you your desires?

How can dysfunction prevent us from getting to God? Dysfunction means that we depart from the norms of social behavior in a way regarded as bad. Oftentimes, our surrounding relationships and self-view can be dysfunctional. When we have lived so long in a dysfunctional point of view, it's hard to recognize, hard to face, and even harder to get out of. Are you staying in relationships you know aren't producing the good fruits of peace, love, joy, righteousness, and self-control? Do you see yourself as valuable? Do you see yourself the way your Father in heaven sees you? You can identify your desires all day long, but if you aren't willing to face your true dysfunctions then you will never get to your desire.

Do you see yourself as valuable?

If you relax in a dysfunction, you introduce distractions and invite detours into your life. You will find you are never carving out that one-on-one time with God and it becomes less and less of a priority to delight yourself in Him. If you don't delight yourself in God, your heart's desire will not be given.

Evaluate My Three Ds

So here's a challenge! I want you to evaluate your dysfunctions, distractions, and detours. Identify the relationships or other things that you have allowed to detour you from your expected purpose, power, and promise. Handle your three Ds so that you can get your three Ps.

Please do not blame other people for the actions you took to relax in your dysfunction. Face yourself. Take personal responsibility for where you are right now so that you are able to forgive yourself and go toward your purpose. You could spend the rest of your life being comfortable in this dysfunction or you could take this challenge so that you can get to your purpose. We talked about this earlier when we discussed who's got your back, but sometimes we can allow the people around us to weigh us down. We can stay within a dysfunction so long that we can't even support ourselves or a God move. So it's time for you to loose yourself from your dysfunction, stop entertaining distractions, and turn around from your detours.

Perhaps you're asking, how do I do that, Cora? What do I do? This is what I did: I created my circle, and I asked myself several questions about my circle, and here it is—a little bit of homework.

1. Are they giving or taking away from me?

2. Do I grow from the things they speak to me?

3. What do they bring to the table?

4. How do I function having them in my life?

5. Are my friends pulling me toward the world or toward God?

"Birds of a feather flock together." How true! When you are able to evaluate your surroundings, then you are able to evaluate you. Hopefully, as you consider these questions, you will be better able to understand the principles behind your morals and core compass. In other words, what makes me tick?

A lot of who we are can be seen by what things and which people we allow in our company. That is why Scripture says to delight yourself in the Lord first. God has this beautiful way of introducing people into our lives, people He wants us to get to know—and not just for our personal benefit. He wants us to bless others too. But if we engage in lengthy times of fellowship with people who aren't seeking God, we will find ourselves drained, distracted, and detoured away from God's central purpose for our lives. Eventually, we will lose the power of God in our lives because we don't really know Him.

When you are able to evaluate your surroundings, then you are able to evaluate you.

It's important that you are walking with God, because when you allow the world to consume you, then you are giving someone else who is willing to walk with Him the access to your gift. Therefore, when you look up and see your idea that you dreamed about being pursued by someone else, you cannot be upset. You would still be with your purpose if you didn't allow toxic environments and toxic people surround you and hold back your power. You must be spiritually strong first so that you can obtain, manage, and walk out your purpose.

Having a vision for purpose, power, and promise doesn't matter if you have no faith to walk it out. Such vision won't matter if you have no God to walk it out with. So make sure you know what you want because you can be so involved in your distractions, detours, and dysfunctions that you birth a stillborn of purpose. You can sit there and hope that you are able to give life, but toxic people in toxic surroundings cannot produce life. However, if you've chosen to step out of those toxic surroundings and walk toward God's purpose for your life, God will meet you.

Today can be a new day. You have picked up this book and you are taking this challenge! You have just been introduced to faithing it in your spirit and you can choose to delight yourself in the Lord from this point forward. You know now that when you delight yourself in the Lord, then and only then can God grant you the desires of your heart. Think about it. To obtain your gift and birth your purpose, you must be willing to be consumed by God more than your dysfunctions.

Delight of My Soul

We talked about dysfunctions, distractions, and detours, so now let's talk about delight. *Delight* means "to please, to give a feeling of happiness." Your life is a testament of what you have done for God. So now we have to ask ourselves, have we fully delighted in the Lord?

Is my life pleasing to God?

What am I delighting in?

Am I pleasing the flesh?

If we please the flesh before Christ, then we can't complain that we don't have our true heart's desires. We must be willing to face the wrong parts and fix them according to God's will.

I told the Lord what I wanted and I lined myself up with Him, using those questions I gave you a few pages back. I gave God my true repentance and got delivered. I want to share more on this a little later, but when I started lining up and voiced my desires, God started placing my steps in a direction where I could walk. He pointed me right toward my promise and my purpose!

Face yourself, forgive yourself, and align yourself.

You can't have everything your heart desires until God is pleased. And in order to please God, you must be willing to face yourself, forgive yourself, and align yourself. Get ready to please God first in all things and crucify your fleshly desires.

Can you truly say that God is pleased right now with your life? This is not just about identifying your desires, but it's about the destination to your desires.

Consume Me, Jesus

So now we get into how to be consumed by Jesus Christ. If we are unable to pray, we are unable to be consumed by Christ. We must be willing to give everything that we are to God. We must be willing to recognize that it is not religion but relationship that God is after. We want to communicate and trust Him with every part of our lives.

Pray that you will love yourself enough to want everything that He has to offer. God wants to consume you, become one with you, become compatible with you! And when you have given Him all of you and you have allowed Him to consume you, then He has become the desire of your heart.

When Jesus Christ consumes you, He consumes your thoughts. Your thoughts are His thoughts! If Jesus consumes you, then you begin to birth your promise. Your surroundings are no longer toxic and you are no longer toxic—what you birth is healthy! Now it's time for you to produce and walk out in purpose so that it can grow, mature, and take over.

When you cleanse your surroundings and your thoughts, you are no longer toxic; rather, you are consumed by God and one with Him. It's so beautiful! You have become one with God and He has changed your name. Think about it. If God can do exceedingly and abundantly above anything you could ever ask or think, then your thoughts are His thoughts. Then you will tap into the fact that your desires have become whatever God thinks of you. His thoughts are higher than your thoughts so your desires for yourself match God's will at this point. Get ready! When you make this step, your blessing will begin to overtake you and God begins to open doors for you. He pours out a blessing in every aspect that you do not have room enough to receive it all. That's why when people first get saved, great things begin to happen and doors begin to open. They are consumed with Christ! If we are consumed with Christ, then we are ready for the world and the attacks. Our belief system is not shaken, and we understand our call. Everything is new and happy because we have been reborn into Christ, into a nontoxic surrounding.

It's possible that later, as a maturing saint, you may have fallen into allowing your toxic surroundings to consume you. And now you are watching other people grow while you have fallen in love with a toxic environment.

"NO MORE!"

NO MORE! I speak to your toxic surrounding and I command it by the power of the Holy Ghost to be gone. I pray right now that you, my friend, be loosed from the captivity of toxic relationships, and that God shift those old friends into position and alignment with His perfect will. I speak to you to be consumed by God Almighty! Let your desires be toward God and of God so that you can break loose from generational curses. I pray right now for you, that you would be free from the yokes of bondage that you became accustomed to and have fallen in love with. I speak liberation in every element of your life! I speak liberation from every spirit that is surrounding you and consuming you that is not of God, both knowingly and unknowingly. You will walk in freedom. You will walk in liberation from this day forward. You will birth purpose, you will birth power, and you will press forward. Today you are reaching, and you will gain power according to God's great power and anointing resting inside of you. It is so and so it is.

Scan this code for Cora's Chapter 5
PRAYER FOR YOU!

Or Visit
WWW.CORAJAKESCOLEMAN.COM

SIX

Paralyzed?
Loose Yourself!

*Ask, and it will be given to you; seek, and you will
find; knock, and it will be opened to you.*

(MATTHEW 7:7)

After we know the dream God wants for our lives, what do we
do after that?

At times we can become frozen in desire. It's like we're paralyzed
and can't move forward. Oftentimes, we are locked in position because we are not able to speak. This is because we have made ourselves
believe that we have no power, but the reality is that the power to be
free from the dead things comes from within us.

Labels can deplete your power and paralyze you! You don't have
to live by the labels that others place on you—you can live by the
labels you speak on yourself.

Has someone told you that your dream is impossible? If you in-
ternalize this negativity and make that your belief, then you will stop

pursuing your gift and progress will be stopped. Believe in yourself and speak life over yourself, otherwise, you will remain in the chains that others spoke on you and you will not be able to loose yourself.

Labels can deplete your power and paralyze you!

Loose Yourself from Lies

So here it is! Are you ready for your first challenge in this chapter? I challenge you to stop living by what others said about you and start speaking God's thoughts over yourself. Don't cry out to people; cry out to God.

Oftentimes, we are paralyzed and unable to get the things we desire because we haven't spoken for ourselves. We haven't believed the power of life and death is in our tongue.

I am the children's ministry director of The Potter's House Church of Dallas now, but when I started I was not the director. I walked into the office with the desire for something bigger than the position I was in, but just as this book says, I had to go through a process. I had to evaluate my support system. I had to start faithing it, and I had to speak it.

So when I walked in the office, I spoke, "I will be the director of this ministry as I have seen it in visions that have been given to me according to God's perfect will and timing." I wasn't the director at the time that I spoke it, but I am the director now. What would have happened if I didn't speak it? I would still be in a mediocre position receiving mediocre praises and getting mediocre pay when God called me to a bigger position than that. I had to speak what I wanted and accept it and go through the process so that I could produce my purpose. Your purpose, power, and promise cannot be obtained without you opening your mouth to speak what you see. Speak out and loose yourself!

As the director, I find that our children believe that they are whatever you speak. So I hear kids tell me:

Don't cry out to people, cry out to God.

- I'm bad.

- I have anger issues.

- I can't do this.

The children truly believe these lies! So often children don't produce life because their parents don't speak life to them. So how does that pertain to who we are now? Whatever was spoken about you as a child will stay with you into adulthood. If your parents spoke life over you, then you experience more freedom than most. If your parents neglected to speak life, then you likely feel paralyzed in certain areas because you believe that what they said all those years ago is actually true. We have to loose ourselves from those lies! For the Bible says this:

> People of Zion, who live in Jerusalem, you
> will weep no more. How gracious He will
> be when you cry for help! As soon as He hears,
> He will answer you (Isaiah 30:19 NIV).

God will answer you and be gracious if *He hears you*, but God can't hear your cry unless *He hears your cry!*

If you don't believe in your dream, no one else will. If you don't believe you have a world-changing purpose, then you won't change the world. Instead, you will be swallowed up by the world that you were supposed to change! Why? Because you were too busy living in what somebody else said. Speak what God's shown you. Speak what you see and desire. If you don't speak up for yourself, then you will be submerged in the bottom of the barrel watching others take the world by storm. You don't want to sit, as the lame man did, on the side of the pool letting people step over you to gain something that could have easily been yours had you wanted it bad enough.

Loose Yourself from Worry

I want to talk to you for a moment about work over worry. Sometimes we can allow ourselves to be consumed by the worry of the timing of our promise, purpose, and power. We become worried about the "when" factor—*when* is God going to make it happen? Worry will rob us of our joy, our peace, and our dream.

Faithing it will take you over the temptation of worry. Let me explain.

You should not worry about when God is going to lift you out of your process and into your purpose. Just stay focused on your work at hand. Faith without works is dead—that's what the Word says! That simply means you have to work for what you believe God for.

My mother-in-law used to always say, "If you are going pray, don't worry. If you are going to worry, don't pray." I love that saying because oftentimes we will pray for something from God but not put effort into the work at hand. So far we've learned that everything we desire to obtain from God is given after we do something. So if you have asked God for something but you are not seeing it manifest, perhaps instead of thinking it's the devil, a spirit, or that you need to fast, perhaps you need to go to work. If you want to see the fruits of your labor, you have to do the work to plant the seed.

If you are going to pray, don't worry. If you are going to worry, don't pray.

Loose Yourself from Laziness

Asking God (prayer) isn't going to get a field planted. You have to go out there and plant the seeds. If you don't, you will look at your surroundings and everyone's field will be producing but yours. In that case, you cannot be upset if the people around you sowed and did the work and they are seeing a harvest, but your field is empty. If you are not willing to sow, then you will not reap. We can stand in our seedless field and worry why it's not growing. In fact, we worry instead of spending our time planting seeds in the field. If you don't want to work, then don't speak, don't ask, and don't knock. Everything you believe God for is going to come with some work, and if you don't want to work really hard to produce a big harvest, then you should not ask for a big purpose. You will receive a big harvest when you are willing to work hard.

The people you see being blessed are receiving an overflow blessing because they sow an overflow of seeds. Do not be jealous of others who are reaping more! Rather, question what you have sown.

The problem is that we often ask for more from God than we are willing to work for or give. So yes, we can worry about the harvest that we aren't receiving, or we can do something else. So here it is—I am giving you another challenge: I challenge you to match the amount of harvest you want to the amount of work you do. Then do as my mother-in-law says: If you are going to pray, don't worry, and if you are going to worry, don't pray.

Jealousy is deadly to the soul and it will stop you from moving forward. It's important that you stop worrying about other people's things and blessings and start working on yourself. A big part of declaring your promise is the understanding that even in declaring what you want you have to put in work. Yes, you want to pray, declare, and decree, but you also have to put in work when you want to obtain anything.

You and I have to put in time at our jobs in order to receive a paycheck. In a relationship, we put in work in order to be fruitful and multiply. Nothing is just handed to you—it is received through hard work.

Loose Yourself from the Past

We all have gone through something that makes us angry and shakes our faith. If we didn't go through something to shake our faith, then God would have never said that faith the size of a mustard seed can move the mountain. Things will shake your faith, but those things have come to bring about the strength in you.

All you have to do is press forward. Stop thinking about why He allowed the rape, molestation, abuse, divorce, abortion, fornication, pregnancy, and so on to happen. Start using the things you overcame to help you declare what is rightfully yours. If you don't go through anything, then you have nothing to talk about. If you have nothing to talk about, then what are you going to ask God for? The power to obtain your promise is based on your ability to embrace the process of the pain.

I know what it's like to be hurt, to be broken, to be bitter, and to be angry. But I decided to speak life to myself and to loose myself from the things that were hindering me. You may have been beaten and you may feel broken, bitter, angry, and hurt, but God has not forgotten about you. You will overcome this! It's time to speak life, and speak out.

When you can speak out about what you've overcome, then the enemy can't use it over you anymore. Your broken self, your bitter self, your negative emotions take power from you. Faith leaves, negativity enters, and you are hindered.

God may have taken you through the storm, but He still gave you a rainbow, and the point is that He took you through it. Start looking at your low points as an opportunity for God to show you His power to bring you out. You will not remain paralyzed at this low point forever! Don't allow your hurt to hinder you from reaching for power; let it motivate you to search for a healer. My dear friend, I speak to you and I say to you without hesitation, "You *can* heal while hurting."

Gain back your power! Overcome the things that are hindering you. When you are able to climb over the rape, the abuse, the humiliation, the embarrassment, the lies, and the hurt, then you will step into your promise.

Loose Yourself from Failure Feelings

I have seen God show up for me even when I didn't deserve it. I believe that you can still be elevated to a high level in Christ even if you don't feel you deserve it. I also believe that the people who stay in that humble vein are the ones who receive the most promotion. It's the people who are willing to withstand the fire who are met by God and then promoted.

Just think about Shadrach, Meshach, and Abednego. They were willing to go into the fire for God because they had faith He would save them. They received great promotion after they withstood the fire, and they were just doing what they felt God would have them to do. God brought them to high promotion because they remained humble and low in spirit (see Daniel 1–3). Your humility will open the doors that pride will close. Moses didn't believe he deserved it, but he stayed humble, and God used him, and God can still use you.

It's the people who are willing to withstand the fire who are met by God and then promoted.

No matter what happened to you, no matter what you went through, God can use you. You don't have to be whole in order for God to use and answer what you declare.

We allow the people who hurt us to take our power, and then we get upset when we are standing powerless, paralyzed, and without direction. Take your power back! Start declaring death on some things and speaking life on other things. What would happen if you were one declaration away from receiving your deliverance? What if all you had to do was speak death on that soul tie, speak death on that sickness, speak death on that past hurt, speak death on that past relationship, and start speaking life on your situation and your circumstances?

God can't bless you if you don't open your mouth. You must first be willing to let go of the weight that is keeping you from leaping into your perfect purpose.

To the people who didn't believe in you? Prove them wrong. You deserve to be at the top of the mountain, just don't get too busy concentrating on the people who have hurt you or surpassed you. Focus on where you are now and work to make it to the top. I am behind you!

God can't bless you if you don't open your mouth.

I want you to know that you *can* reach the top.

I want you to know that you *do* have a gift.

I want you to know that you *are* talented and necessary in the Kingdom.

Prayer—Get Real with God

Prayer got me out of my situation. I found true freedom when I communicated with God. I was real, open, and vulnerable with the only person who knows everything about me today, and everything about where I am going. Prayer allowed me the opportunity to talk to God—to speak to Him, to tell Him about my hurt, my pain, and my anger. If you can't be real with God about the things that hurt you and anger you, then you aren't having a real relationship. We always get in this stigma of saying we aren't supposed to ask God why. I don't know why we tell people that, because when Jesus was suspended on the cross, pierced in His hands and feet, He looked up at His Father and said something. The Bible says in Mark 15:34, "And at three in the afternoon Jesus cried out in a loud voice, 'Eloi, Eloi, lema sabachthani?' (which means 'My God, My God, why have You forsaken Me?')" (NIV).

Jesus was in relationship with God His Father. He felt connected to Him, and we too should have the same connection. God is your Father. If you don't know what's going on, if you want to ask your Daddy a question, then you ask Him. Don't sit in your anger and bitterness because you are afraid to ask God why. It is through our inability to connect with God in communication that the enemy is able to destroy us. Take your true self to God without hesitation! Go to Him in spirit and in truth, then you will have a breakthrough that will change your life for the better.

You deserve to have a relationship with your Father God. And if you know God better, in turn you will know *you* better. In fact, this is how you tap into the thing that makes you royalty! The God who healed the blind, raised the dead, and turned water into wine is the same miracle-working God in you. Also, while you're talking to your Father, ask Him for a strategy to help you produce your purpose. It takes more than just speaking it as you know, but you also need strategy, you need a plan, and you then need to walk it out.

You can get your power back! Go before the Lord with your anger and allow Him to heal you so that you are able to push forward in what He has for you.

Write a Letter to God

Are you carrying your cross and going through turmoil? Do you feel beaten and crushed? Even paralyzed? This is the perfect time to look to Him.

This is what I want you to do. I want you to write a letter to God, asking Him, "Why?" But listen to me, I want you to ask Him why from your hurt and broken place. When I went before God with my why it was, "Why would You make me go through infertility? Why would You allow them to hurt me?" I had several whys, but I ended my letter telling God my truth. This was my truth to Him: "God, I'm hurting and I'm angry. I love You and I want to trust You, but I am scared, and I need to know why I had to go through all this beating and all this crushing? I know You love me more than this, Lord. Help me to have faith in Your ability to give me everything I'm believing You for, even though I am hurt from what You allowed me to endure."

I received my answer, and I'm praying you will receive yours as well. God has a strategy and a plan for you, but you can't have access to the room until you are willing to address your situation.

What Am I Talking About?

God created the world all from the words that came from His mouth. God showed us that in order for us to produce greatness we must connect to the power that we have in our mouths. We can obtain whatever we speak while in relationship with God! How do I know? The Bible tells me so!

> *Ask and it will be given to you; seek and you will find; knock and the door will be opened to you* (Matthew 7:7 NIV).

We sometimes allow ourselves to stay in bondage and not have what is rightfully ours. All of this bondage is unnecessary. Speak to the mountain. Ask. Seek. Knock. If you want to obtain the thing that God has for you, speak it out. You have no more excuses! You have reached the point of knowing that you have to speak what you want to produce.

Ask and receive. Your purpose is of no value if it isn't spoken for. A lot of us have promises and purposes waiting for us, but we are unable to obtain them because we simply haven't opened our mouths. We haven't knocked on the door. We haven't declared our promise to come forth. So, what are you talking about? Are you wasting your words on something besides your God-given dream?

Everything that unlocks our blessings comes from our mouths. Let's look at another Scripture:

> *Again, truly I tell you that if two of you on earth agree about anything they ask for, it will be done for them by My Father in heaven* (Matthew 18:19 NIV).

To *ask* means "to say something in order to obtain an answer or some information." There it is again—*say something*. If you don't speak you can't obtain. If you allow yourself to be tongue-tied by the webs of the enemy, you will stay paralyzed—and you can't be upset when you don't have what is rightfully yours. Speak out! Don't allow people to speak for you. Speak for yourself. Part of bringing purpose back to life is to speak life.

Declare your promise, declare your power, and loose yourself from the entanglements of the world. Start labeling yourself according to what God thinks about you. Open your mouth so you can obtain your victory, promise, and power. It's in your mouth! Victory is in your mouth. If you don't decree and declare your vision, then it can't come to pass. In this moment you must understand that you are a child of the King, therefore you have rights to Kingdom blessings. But you must go through the pain of the process and embrace it and start declaring things over yourself.

Are you wasting your words on something besides your God-given dream?

You are linked to greatness—Jesus Christ. Therefore, you deserve greatness, but not without great struggles. Be delivered from your pain. Speak over yourself, address yourself, gain real relationship with Christ, and leap into your destiny and walk it out.

I Tell You, Arise

I am speaking to the scared you who is afraid to speak life because of the fear of what your success looks like in God's eyes. I speak to you, and I tell you, "Arise my king, queen, prince, princess. Arise. You were born to be great. You are an heir to the King of kings. You have a lot to offer, and you have a lot to give. You can do it. Pursue your dream. Press through. Whatever you do, don't let failure stop you—let it push you. Whatever you do don't let downfalls keep you from going up the hill. You are royalty, you own the light, and you choose whether you will rest in the light or settle in the darkness." So I take this time to speak and declare life over your purpose and your promise.

You are royalty, you own the light.

I pray that God places a heart in you that seeks Him with all that you have. I pray that God ignites the power within you to bring forth the things that He has spoken over your life. I pray that God restores you from the pain that you allowed to consume you. I pray God removes the weight that hinders you from being able to leap into your purpose. I pray that the pain of the past not be an issue for you, but that you use the past pains to press you forward. I pray that God would break every generational curse that you have accepted and that you haven't accepted, which has tried to bind you, and we curse it at the root. I pray that the fire of God seals every area of your life that is aligned with His perfect will and purpose for you. I pray that you would press forward and begin to speak life to the areas that need to be brought back to life and speak death to the bad areas that need to be dead. You are to be great in your purpose! I pray you begin to open your mouth and work and that the minute you do your harvest be plentiful and overflowing. I thank God that you are walking into your purpose with power, and that you are faithing it from this day forward. Thank you, God, it is so and so it is. Amen!

Scan this code for Cora's Chapter 6
PRAYER FOR YOU!

Or Visit
WWW.CORAJAKESCOLEMAN.COM

Faithing It

SEVEN

Believe God

Surely God is my salvation; I will trust and not be afraid. The Lord, the Lord Himself, is my strength and my defense; He has become my salvation.

(Isaiah 12:2 NIV)

*B*elief is defined as "trust, faith, or confidence in someone or something." *Trust* is defined as "a firm belief in the reliability of something." Why is this important? Because we must be able to put our trust in God. What happens with us is that we can rely on people to handle things, and we end up putting our trust in people instead of God. God wants us to trust in Him over our own friends, coworkers, and even our own thoughts.

Without trust in God you are bound to the trust that you place in man, and humanity will fail you every time. How do we know trusting in the Lord is so important? Let's go back to the Word. The Bible says, "Trust in the Lord with all your heart and lean not on your own understanding" (Proverbs 3:5 NIV). We must be able to trust in God over our own thoughts, theories, perceptions, concerns, and understanding. If I decide to believe God is bigger than me and better than me, and I allow Him to consume me, then my thoughts are His—and God has great thoughts about me! God sees me better than I could ever see myself.

God sees my ugly self and He still uses me.

God see the things I am embarrassed about and He still uses me.

God sees the times I didn't trust He was going to do it for me, and He still uses me.

And guess what? If God can still use me, then He can still use you. God is more reliable than any man or woman we know. On the other hand, there are relationships that God ordains and brings together. We carry a measure of trust with people that we know God brought into our lives. That's a good thing, and hopefully those God-ordained relationships will help us to stop putting faith and trust in relationships of the world. Put your trust in the relationships God has ordained and brought together. You are in charge of your fate and your faith. Push for it! Believe God for the things you want to obtain. You are powerful when you rely on God.

God has great thoughts about me!

Trust God First

You must be able to trust God first—that is the first step in our definition of belief in God. If you don't believe God is able to do more than you can, or more than humanity can, then you will not produce at a higher level. To trust people more than God is to allow yourself to have trust and belief in a flawed person and a flawed system. When you put your trust in a flawed thing, then you cannot expect that to produce a beautiful outcome.

The only person who can turn ashes into beauty is God. God is the Creator of all things, and He is the only One you can trust to turn your flaws into something that can be used flawlessly.

You may have broken pieces in your life, but let me encourage you to stop giving them to a person to fix. Start giving them to God so that He can turn your broken into beautiful. It's easy to give up, but I don't want you to give up. I want you to trust God to turn your ashes into beautiful. We must recognize that God is our artist and we just need to give Him our paintbrush. We must trust in the Lord.

The only person that can turn ashes into beauty is God.

Have Faith

The next step in our definition of *belief* is to have faith. We talked a lot about faith in chapter 2, but I want to talk to you about it on the perspective of the literal definition, not the biblical definition of faith. There is more to faith than just our biblical perspective.

When we look up the meaning of *faith*, it is defined as "trust or confidence in someone or something." What does that really mean—to have confidence in something? To have confidence in someone is the state of feeling certain about the truth of something. So if we have trust, we must now have faith, and in having faith we have linked up with confidence as well.

It's hard to understand that God can do more for you than you can do for yourself. To ensure the fulfillment of your purpose and promise, you must be willing to believe God even when it's hard. And in order to believe God, you must trust, accept, and have faith and confidence in His ability to get the victory over your situation. Without belief in God, we can't produce.

Faith in Me or Faith in God?

Now that we went over the definition of belief, I want to talk about your heart. We can't really believe God if we don't have a heart for Him, especially if we don't have a heart for His ability. Sometimes the way to show God we believe Him is to trust Him with the thing we have held in our heart and hands all along. The purpose and plan God has for us is bigger and better than what we could have thought. Ever since I was a little girl, I dreamed of my own little boy named Nehemiah, and I held on to him almost religiously. I began to write to him and dream about him. I brought life to my dream, and when I was diagnosed with infertility I just held on to my dream even tighter. I made myself the dream catcher by any means necessary.

Until one day God said, "Give him to Me." I had gone through two in vitro fertilization (IVF) cycles at this point. I was scared that he wasn't going to come. I had done all the fertility treatments, vitamins, acupuncture, teas, and herbs. I had a lot of belief in my ability, and I trusted my ability. I had confidence in the articles I read, and I was doing everything that the world told me to do, but I was too afraid to give God my dream. I felt like if I gave up the fight and I let Nehemiah go, then I had let the devil win. I didn't understand at the time that it was my belief in myself and confidence in me that caused me to continue to lose the fight.

I didn't understand that I believed more in the information I received from the world than I did in what God showed me. God doesn't give you a vision or a dream of your purpose for you to snatch it from Him and make it happen for yourself! God gave you the vision so that you could see what He was capable of—not what you were supposed to grab, but what He was going to grab for you. What if I were to tell you that the reason you haven't gotten your promise is because you have turned your dream into an idol over God, and God has become jealous? That is highly possible! You know, until you give God back His dream for you and take your hands off of it, you won't be able to get what was supposed to be yours a long time ago. Your belief in self is going to stop you from obtaining what God wants to give you.

Give the Vision Back to God

Here is your first challenge in this chapter. It may sound similar to ones we have done before, but this comes from the very soul and heart of you. This one may be painful and breaking, but it's going to bring you a release that is strong and necessary in order for you to walk in your calling. Here it is: surrender.

Believing God is not just something that you hear, it's something that you do. It's a release of self. This kind of belief comes with your ability to say and feel, "I surrender all." You have to be able to believe God is better, God is stronger, and He is your defense. Remember, "The Lord, the Lord Himself, is my strength and my defense; He has become my salvation" (Isaiah 12:2 NIV).

Let me explain how this worked for me. I had to give Nehemiah to God and stand on my belief in God over myself. I understand that if God said I would birth a son, then I would birth a son and it would be according to His perfect will and purpose for me. Even if He wasn't to give me Nehemiah, as I have dreamed, I recognize that whatever God has for me is better than anything I could orchestrate myself. Again, all of this brings me to the Scripture at the beginning of this chapter:

"I surrender all."

> *Surely God is my salvation; I will trust and not be afraid. The Lord, the Lord Himself, is my strength and my defense; He has become my salvation* (Isaiah 12:2 NIV).

I Will Not Be Afraid

My favorite part of our Scripture is exactly what I was telling all of us before. Isaiah says, "I will trust and not be afraid." Let's stop there.

It's important that when you make a decision to believe (trust) God, you do it without fear. Oftentimes, we are not receiving the full promise and purpose that God has for us because we are too afraid to let go. We fear what will happen if we turn everything over to God. We fear what will happen if we don't keep our hands on our own vision. But this is God's vision! And God's vision doesn't operate by our own will and desires! What will happen if you stop believing in yourself and start trusting in God? If God gave you the vision, then He can create what He gave. Sometimes your promise is delayed because you won't deliver your vision back to God.

Now catch this—your true salvation comes in your trusting God without fear. True salvation means your deliverance from sin and its consequences, but also the preservation or deliverance from harm, ruin, or loss. This great salvation is ours—without fear.

God became Isaiah's salvation after he decided to trust in the Lord without fear. God needs you to trust Him without fear and without hesitation. Let go of what you have and give it to God. Your purpose and power doesn't belong to you, it is given through your trust and belief in God. That's what we have been talking about this whole time. You need to trust God again and develop a relationship and submission to God so that you can obtain that vision, dream, and plan He has for you. This is not the final step, but if you choose to take this step God will open the doors, and He will save you. You will learn the power of God's ability when you recognize how power-less you are without His ability.

Submission to the Holy Spirit can be hard, but I say to you: Don't be your own hindrance. Surrender! Don't spend any more time holding on to your life and operating in your own will. Hand it over to God. Surrender yourself to God's passion for you. I know you've been hurt and I know that you are angry. I know that you are afraid of letting go. Yes, it's hard to say, "God, even if You don't give it to me, I'll be satisfied." And I know the world's opinions and statements are trying to micromanage your faith.

I know it's hard to let go and trust God because you are trying to figure out where He is and why He hasn't opened the door and brought you what He promised you. The answer is simple. You can't believe in God's ability while making a backup plan in case He doesn't perform to your liking. You can't make a backup plan to God's timing because His timing is perfect. You are either going to operate in God's will or you will stand in your own will, but let me warn you: If you are not prospering in purpose it is because you are powerless, and you are powerless because you haven't allowed yourself to have an encounter and a trust in something that's bigger than you. If you aren't growing in God, it's because you have decided to grow in yourself.

You are either going to operate in God's will or you will stand in your own will.

I Am Responsible for Me

For your second challenge, I challenge you to stop resenting God for the pain you went through and release your hands off your situation.

Jesus endured the pain, suffering, and crushing, and He didn't complain. You have to understand that God is for you.

Jesus gave His life because He was *for* you.

Jesus was beaten because He was *for* you.

Jesus was nailed because He was *for* you.

And He didn't command them to stop tormenting Him because He was *for* you. If you don't stop blaming Him for your crushing and beating and start believing that He is for you, then you won't reach your full potential. Even when Adam and Eve sinned, He covered them up because He was *for* them.

We are spending more time complaining about the beating and not understanding that God never complained. We are more for ourselves than for God.

When we see that we aren't producing, we get mad. Really, all we need to do is believe that God is better at operating our story than we are. Therefore the enemy controls us because he discovers that we don't trust enough in God to believe that He is able to pull us through. We were never meant to fight the enemy, we were meant to resist him. We are to use our faith to defeat the enemies we have created within ourselves because we don't believe that God is greater than our weapons and more powerful than our floods.

You know what I mean—that thing you can fall into where everything that happens is the devil or a spirit. Yeah, you know what I'm talking about. It's that thing where you don't take responsibility for where you are, and how you ended up at a dead end in life. You simply make it the devil's fault so that you don't have to be responsible.

We must believe that God is better at living our lives and controlling our lives than we are. Otherwise, we will take the control and operate our vision, and we do everything on our own instead of believing God. This battle is not yours; it is the Lord's. It's time for you to take responsibility for where you are and turn it over to God and let Him navigate you through your obstacles of life.

It's simple, really. We can't do things the wrong way and expect God to bless it the right way. We can't trust ourselves more than we trust God. Here's a question: Where is your belief?

Have you been drowning and don't know why? Have you been challenging God and giving Him ultimatums and then getting upset when He doesn't pick the choice you wanted Him to? Believing God doesn't come with you giving Him ultimatums.

We can't do things the wrong way and expect God to bless it the right way.

Here's an ultimatum for all of us: Believe God or don't believe God, but don't live your life one way and then expect God to make moves for you. You are responsible for how you are blessed, just as the Scripture says when you trust (believe), God becomes your salvation. In order to be saved from the hurts and damages of the world, you must trust God.

Trust and Believe God in the Darkness

I know what you are saying—it's easier said than done. Let me share a story with you. I have a friend named Jada. She and her husband, Darryl, had been married for some time when naturally they wanted to start a family. They are both completely dedicated to God, financially stable, spiritually stable, and believing God with everything they had. They were ready and had everything planned and set up, but weeks turned into months and months turned into a year, and several negative pregnancy tests later they were faced with the devastating news from the doctor that they would not be able to conceive without a lot of help. So they began the journey of hoping and still believing God but also having to go to specialists and doing fertility treatments. They fasted and prayed. All the while they watched the people around them getting pregnant while they prayed and hoped for their child to come to pass.

Thoughts plagued their minds. *What did we do wrong? Are we being punished? Why is this happening to us?* They experienced the devastation of wanting to be happy for that friend who got pregnant but still desiring the same thing to happen to them. Though the weight of the pain got heavy and there were nights they cried, they never stopped believing God. They never doubted God's ability. They never left God. They trusted God. They were pushing for conception but continuously getting nos from God. Yet a year and four months later, when Jada was about to undergo another fertility treatment route, she'd always answer her phone by saying, "I believe God," instead of saying hello.

She was sitting across from her husband at her favorite restaurant enjoying some seafood when suddenly, after eating her favorite meal, she got nauseous. Her husband looked at her and he knew immediately their belief in God had finally paid off. He knew immediately that they made the right decision in trusting God. He knew immediately that although they went through the pain, God still covered them. It was in that moment he knew that he and Jada would be expecting their first blessing.

That day was the first time Jada took a pregnancy test and did not cry tears of pain. This time as the lines began to pop up on the test, she overflowed in tears. Her heart was full, excited, and indescribable emotions were inside her. Her husband, Darryl, makes this chapter and this story complete. When hearing the news he immediately fell to his knees and began to thank God. They went through the pain, they suffered the crushing, but they never stopped believing God. Even when they did not receive their promise, they believed God. And after they received their promise, they thanked God.

Previously, the doctors said they would never have children without medical help. Today they have three beautiful children all given to them through natural conception. God doesn't need outside sources to give you a blessing. Everything you need to accomplish your promise is in you. Your faith and trust in God, even when you aren't holding your promise, is the thing that brings your promise forth. Jada and Darryl believed God when they were breaking and hurting. They believed and trusted God, and because they withstood their storm they were blessed with the rainbow.

Faith in the darkness is very much like Daniel in the lion's den. Daniel was dropped into the den of lions by his enemies, yet he had no fear—only faith and belief in God's capability. Daniel believed in God more than he believed in his ability to fight the lions, and he was saved (see Daniel 6). So I say this to you: You may be standing in the lion's den and you may have been wrongfully thrown in, but if you will stand on faith, you will be saved.

The promise is coming! You are just in the waiting room. God is preparing your room and He is making the pathway straight. Don't complain in your waiting room; prepare yourself for what you are about to walk into.

Wait without Whining

Don't complain in your waiting room; prepare in your waiting room. There's no point in asking God to shift some things in your life and to make the crooked paths straight and then get upset when He says wait. Sometimes it's not God saying no to you, it's not even God saying it's not going to happen. Sometimes God is just sitting you in the waiting room while He is preparing a place for you.

Are you willing to wait without whining? I promise you, if you wait without whining your reward will be worth the wait. You are a treasure to God, and your promise and purpose can't just be given to you quickly, it has to be prepared.

Daniel had to wait for someone to open the door in the lion's den.

The woman with the issue of blood had to wait for Jesus to pass by.

Jada and Darryl had to wait for their baby.

None of these people complained. They believed and even worshiped God in their waiting. What you do while you are waiting is entirely up to you, but what you do while you are waiting will decide how big your room is. If you rush your blessing and push God's blessing, then you will miss out on lessons you could have learned while you were waiting. You may even miss out on the blessings

Are you willing to wait without whining?

that you could gain if you would sit down and wait on God instead of doing things the way you think they should be done.

The beautiful thing about waiting is that after you are done waiting without complaining, your reward is great. God wants you to hold your peace and wait for Him to claim the victory over your circumstance.

You don't have to be tormented.

You don't have to be bothered.

You don't have to worry.

You don't have to look around.

You don't even have to ask others how long they had to wait.

Your room may be bigger than the person next to you, so it takes more time for it to be prepared. So of course we aren't talking about a literal waiting room, we are talking about a spiritual waiting room. The way my father says it is, "A delay is not a denial." We can spend too much time on the denial and not enough on the delay. Just because you have been delayed in receiving your promise doesn't mean you have been denied. You are just being delayed.

Worship in the Waiting

Worship in your delay so that God can deliver your promise and purpose in a big room that has been specifically prepared for you. What is inside of you is extraordinary, and when you start understanding that then you will be able to recognize the beauty of the waiting. Quite honestly, the longer you have to wait, the bigger your room, the bigger your purpose, and the greater your promise. People who don't go through a waiting period have a smaller purpose. You have been called to something bigger than yourself, and with that comes a huge responsibility and you must take that seriously.

Your wisdom is in the waiting. Your knowledge, peace, and joy are in the waiting. Your strength to endure whatever you are about to be given is in the waiting.

Embrace your waiting room so that you can gain all the things you need in order to overcome the challenges of life. I've sat in the waiting room. God has opened the door in some areas, but in other areas I am still waiting. In some areas I am still gaining the tools I need to become great, but I have learned to be quiet, to trust the Lord, and be still in the waiting room.

God is a better friend and confidant than anyone. While you are waiting, pray and stay strong and seek God in all matters. You are in good company. God has His hands on you and He is preparing your room—all you have to do is wait. God will open the door and He is going to call your name. He hasn't forgotten about you; He was just preparing you and preparing your path.

Embrace your waiting room.

Walk forward, my dear. Believe in God. Be strong in the Lord and in the power of His might. Put on your full armor so that you can stand against the devil's schemes—you have the ability to stand against the tactics and plans of the enemy. The road has been tough, but do not be weary.

You've been broken, but believe God.

You've been waiting, but believe God.

You have felt alone, but believe God.

Your hope will birth your promise if you let God be your doctor. Trust in the Lord and have faith. Walk in your purpose. I know what it's like to feel lost and confused, but the answer is in your belief. May God strengthen your belief! Let me pray for you right now.

> *I pray that your faith be strong and that you believe God more. I pray that you leave the old you and trust the new you, and that your desire for God grows and flourishes in a way like it never has before. I pray that you are lifted from the bottom, and that you push for the top. You have all power in your hands when you are holding God's hand. I pray that you would take God's hand and that God would lead you to virtue and that you would rise to leadership.*
>
> *I pray that you find strength in your sadness, and that you would build your happiness in the midst of your brokenness. I pray that the Lord would be your guide and your light in a dark place. I pray that God consumes you from the crown of your head to the soles of your feet, that God will strengthen your bravery, your wisdom, and your understanding.*
>
> *I pray that the gifting in you that you have yet to discover would pour out, and I pray that God gives you a heart to forgive those who have wronged you knowingly and unknowingly. More importantly, God, I pray that You would heal the heart of my friend right now and that You would help them to forgive themselves and to understand Your heart*

for them. You are the author of our fate and in that we do trust. I thank You, God, for all You are going to do for this person and all that You have already done. Amen and amen.

Scan this code for Cora's Chapter 7
PRAYER FOR YOU!

Or Visit
WWW.CORAJAKESCOLEMAN.COM

Faithing It

EIGHT

There is Power in the No!

But He said to me, "My grace is sufficient for you, for My power is made perfect in weakness." Therefore I will boast all the more gladly about my weaknesses, so that Christ's power may rest on me.

(2 CORINTHIANS 12:9 NIV)

One reason why I wrote this book is because it gives me the opportunity to boast about my hard times and my weaknesses. Today, I want to share with you my hard places and brag on God's ability to take over and be strong in the areas where I am weak.

What's funny about being a Christian is that God can say no to you when you're doing everything right. For example, I was praying and in ministry and I asked God for something that I wasn't quite ready for. I thought I was ready, but God knew that I wasn't. And when He told me no, instead of facing my weaknesses I made excuses for my downfalls.

From my point of view, I was doing everything right. I made my checklist. I am a child of God, I delight myself in God, and I am daily delivering myself from myself. I wake up in the morning saying, "God, I am an open vessel for You to use for Your perfect will and glory." So even after doing all of that and living an "upright life," God still tells me no!

God can say no to you when you're doing everything right.

When I would hear no from God, it would make my flesh weak. My weaknesses came to the forefront and I swept them under the rug. I wouldn't talk about the fact that I had flaws and weaknesses. It was hard until I figured out why. I wouldn't talk about the hurts I was experiencing. I would live the life that everyone wanted me to live.

Instead of telling people the truth, I boasted about the things that made me strong and great. I wouldn't dare let anyone know that I was broken and hurting. I was leading but I was bleeding because I had never seen anyone great show me their weak areas.

Today I know I don't have to be perfect to help you achieve purpose.

I don't have to act like I am strong; I can share my weaknesses.

I don't have to be whole to help you reach your goal.

In fact, I gladly say that I have weaknesses because God has given me strength in my weaknesses. God has given me direction in my depression and power with my passion and my purpose. And though I may not have my promise in my hand, and though I may not have yet conceived, I know God has planted a seed in me. As long as I am real with God, then I can show some realness to you. Then I can bring life to this promised seed He has planted.

The Power of No

The concept of this chapter is very dear to my heart because today I understand why God said no at times in my life. God's no makes so much more sense to me now than it did when He said no the first time.

I was leading but I was bleeding because I had never seen anyone great show me their weak areas.

There are many ways God says no. God can say no, not now, absolutely not, no no no no, etc. It actually reminds me of a "no" button that my mother gave me for Christmas one year. It had many different ways to say no. I loved that button until I realized that I was hearing no from God in several different ways.

I am a weak producer without God. I don't have to worry about that now because God is my producer, my strength, my Father, my mentor, my disciplinarian, my leader, my everything. When I worship Him, I show God the weakest sides of myself in that moment. Still, He knows that He is my everything and I am faithing it in all my weakest places. I show God my love, my faith, and my worship while I'm in the doctor's office, in the waiting room, in the bathroom, and on the floor in the closet. The only way I can be a faither is through God. I do not walk in my own strength; I walk in God's strength and power because I understand I am nothing without the power and blood of Jesus.

Here it is. Even if God doesn't do anything else for you, He has already done enough! When you acknowledge Him in all your weakest places, you show Him that He holds the power. This is about you showing God that you believe He can fix your broken pieces.

So here's your challenge for this chapter: I challenge you to begin showing God how much you trust, believe, and have faith in Him. I want you to do this by expressing your testimony even if He hasn't given you complete victory yet. I want to challenge you to share your story with the next person you see. Show somebody that God is the strength in your weakness.

Your Alabaster Moment

Another word for weakness is *vulnerability*. I want you to begin to show God that you want to be vulnerable toward Him, whether or not you have it all together or not. One day while Jesus was eating with friends, a woman came into the dining room with expensive perfume and lavishly poured out all of that treasure on Jesus' head. Let's look at the story in the Bible:

> *While He was eating, a woman came in with a beautiful alabaster jar of expensive perfume and poured it over His head. The disciples were indignant when they saw this. "What a waste!" they said. "It could have been sold for a high price and the money given to the poor."*

But Jesus, aware of this, replied, "Why criticize this woman for doing such a good thing to Me? You will always have the poor among you, but you will not always have Me. She has poured this perfume on Me to prepare My body for burial. I tell you the truth, wherever the Good News is preached throughout the world, this woman's deed will be remembered and discussed" (Matthew 26:7–13 NLT).

And so it is. We are talking about her deed right now in this book. I think that this woman knew that she was opening herself up for rebuke when she walked into the dining room. I think that she knew she was making herself vulnerable to be attacked, but it didn't stop her. She brought to Jesus her most expensive gift and poured it out on Him. She wasn't looking for a blessing, she was looking to bless.

This is your alabaster moment. You need to pour out to God your hurts and bitter circumstances. Make yourself vulnerable to God and show Him that you believe that His power is the only power that can claim the victory over your finances, your relationship, your pain, your story, your household, your job, and your purpose. Show God that even if you have nothing, you believe He deserves what little you do have. If you have financial weakness, then stand before God in that weakness and boast gladly to the Lord, saying, "God, I may not have anything, but what I do have belongs to you. Even if I haven't figured out a way, I know You will make a way."

Give God Access

Sometimes God gives us a no because we gave Him a no to our money, a no to the foundation of our relationship, a no to our home, a no to our children, a no to our tithes, a no to our purpose, a no to our promise, or a no to our call.

Ask yourself this: Are you asking God for a yes to your prayer when you didn't give Him a yes to His call? Have you held your hands *out* for "more please" than you have held your hands *up* to say thank You? Are you personally giving your treasure, time, and talent into the house of God? Here's the big one: Do you give God money? If you are not giving your money, your time, and your talents into the body of Christ, then you are limiting your access to your power because you are limiting God's access to your life.

Are you asking God for a yes to your prayer when you didn't give Him a yes to His call?

If I walk into your house, will your life show me a life that God could say yes to or is your life for God just something people can see in church? If your life doesn't show a yes to God, then don't expect Him to show a yes to you. God's power gets all access to every door. You can't knock on the door and ask God to answer it when He's not in your foundation.

Listen to me. How dare we feel entitled to God giving us a yes when we haven't given Him a yes. Show your yes! Do more than act it—say it, show it, and prove it. If you say yes to God's call, then He will say yes to you. How do I know? The Bible says:

> "Bring all the tithes into the storehouse, that there may be food in My house, and try Me now in this," says the Lord of hosts, "if I will not open for you the windows of heaven and pour out for you such blessing that there will not be room enough to receive it" (Malachi 3:10).

When you give to God, He gives to you. When you reach for God, He will reach for you. Now catch this—God doesn't have to say yes to you. It's a privilege to get a yes from God. You are empowered in that. How awesome that you would say yes to God, and He would consider you enough to say yes back! Don't make God regret His yes, and don't get mad if He says no. You don't know why He said no, so wait and continue to share and make God the foundation and the truth in your weakness so that He can strengthen you and give you His power.

As children of the King, it is important to understand that we will have times where we will not be given what we want right away, and we may reach for something that looks exciting and fun for us, but God will say no because He knows more than we do. You can live life reaching for the things that aren't meant to be yours or you can heed to God's instruction. Sometimes our goals are not stronger and higher than God. Naturally we want to know why God doesn't allow us to have the things that we want when we want them. I am so glad to have the opportunity to give you some peace about God's no!

I'm Okay with No

We must realize that sometimes God will say no. And we need to be okay with that. We must be careful to not treat God as a genie whom we expect to perform every time we fall to our knees in prayer. Did your earthly father perform like that for you and give you every little thing you asked for? I hope not!

We don't ask God for things and expect Him to just say yes every time. Sometimes, you will ask God a question and He is evaluating whether what you asked for is better than what He has for you.

Imagine this: Your child asks you if she can go to the park on Friday, but she doesn't realize that you have a surprise trip to Disney World planned for her that weekend. She may be disappointed in your no but that's because she doesn't see what you have planned yet. If you complain because of the no then you won't be open to receive what God has, and what God has is always better than what you planned. When we delight ourselves in God, trust Him, go through the process, and embrace the pain, we will experience healing and naturally soar into the passion of our purpose. We can still ask God for things. The only thing is that now when you ask you are asking as a whole and healed person, someone who delights in God and is determined to walk in God's will, not your own will.

It may still hurt when you ask for something and God says no. You try to figure out why. You try to understand where He is coming from, but it's hard when you are awaiting His next move.

The worst part of walking in God's will is that you don't know His next move. But that's okay because when you are walking in God's will, His next move is always better than what you thought of without Him. I want you to be okay with your no. God doesn't just say no because He doesn't want you to have what you want, but God says no for several reasons. Let's look at those reasons now.

Why Does God Say No?

The first reason God says no sometimes is actually the hardest to accept. Even though we may be walking in God's will, we may not be prepared for what He has for us. We are quick to ask for things to fill the void and pain in our hearts, but we may not be ready yet for what God is going to give us.

It's possible that we have asked for a husband or a wife, but we aren't prepared to be a husband or a wife in return. Perhaps we ask for the management position, but we still have a low-income mindset. We can ask for a house, but we don't have income to manage the house. It doesn't matter what you asked for, what matters is if you are ready for what you asked for. Are you walking in faith? Does your life match what you are asking for? If I look at your life will I see that you are ready for what you are asking for from the Lord?

Let me put it like this. I was praying for God to bring me a baby and to allow me to be fruitful and multiply, but I wasn't taking prenatal vitamins, I wasn't working out, I wasn't drinking water, and I wasn't preparing my body to receive what I was asking for. So when I jumped in my own will to pursue what I wanted, God said no. At the time I got upset and I was hurt and angry, but I didn't realize that I wasn't prepared to receive what I was asking for.

I was crying out for a husband, but I wasn't learning how to cook, I wasn't enjoying cleaning, and I wasn't healed from my past relationships. So this is what I am saying: Show God that you are ready to receive what you ask Him for. Show God that you aren't just an asker, but you are a doer. You're not defined by what you say and ask for, but you are defined by what you do to get what you ask for. Your promise is given after hard work.

The second reason why God could possibly say no to our prayers is easier for me to understand. He has something better for us. It could be that you prepared and prayed and God still said no. The answer to this is hard to believe, especially for those of us who can be a bit controlling! God has written something better for you. Trust Him to write your book! There is no need to go into this big explanation here. God is for us, and He wants us to win. He wants us to have the victory.

Sufficient Grace

Trust God that when you are weak, His power takes over—which brings up our Scripture for this chapter. Let's break it down.

> *But He said to me, "My grace is sufficient for you, for My power is made perfect in weakness." Therefore I will boast all the more gladly about my weaknesses, so that Christ's power may rest on me* (2 Corinthians 12:9 NIV).

We must understand grace. We have talked about faith, trust, belief, and even love, but we haven't talked about grace. Biblically, we know that grace is sufficient and it's new every morning, but what does it mean to really have grace? Well, let me tell you: Grace is a virtue that comes from God. Now, that is a bit vague, so let's go a little deeper. The word *virtue* means "a behavior showing high moral standards." So don't complain about your problems when you are weak. Maintain your high moral standards and yield your trust in God's grace—*God's* ability to bring His power and His strength into your weakness.

God beckons us to have grace in our hard times because His strength is made perfect in weakness. After God tells him this, Paul writes down that he will now boast about his weaknesses! Now isn't that crazy? Why in the world would anyone want to boast about their weakness? It's because in our weakness God's strength is made perfect. So maintain your morals and standards as you cry out to God for His grace so that you can receive power in your weakness.

Why is that important? When we go through storms in life and when things get heavy and we don't know what to do, we often begin to complain and ask Him to free us from our bondage. We want the ability to fight back, and we want Him to loose us, but if we will begin to boast in our weakness, then and only then will God be able to consume us with power. You have to go through your weakest points in order for God to give you power. So instead of us complaining about our weaknesses and wanting to be taken out of the weak areas, we must embrace them and boast about them. In doing so, we are seeking for strength that is higher than our strength.

You will be great! You will come forth and obtain the power you need, but don't run from the no. And don't be angry when God says no, trust His no so that you can gain His power.

I can remember model Tyra Banks saying that she received several nos from agencies before she got a yes. She didn't let the no stop her. She let the weakness and pain from receiving the no push her, and because she embraced the no and accepted it, she gained power. She gained promotion, purpose, power, and position. The position of your power comes at the level of your ability to boast about your weakness.

The position of your power comes at the level of your ability to boast about your weakness.

That's the thing about the no. When you have gone through the process, said your prayers, gained the relationship with God, and delighted yourself in Him, then when God says no it puts you in a weak place. But remember, God has answered your weakness and given you strength.

What I enjoy about our Scripture, is that if you go to chapter ten of Second Corinthians, Paul tells us how to feel about our weaknesses. He tells us what position we should rest in when we are going through ridicule in the world and others are being blessed and we aren't. Let's look at this:

> *That is why, for Christ's sake, I delight in weaknesses, in insults, in hardships, in persecutions, in difficulties. For when I am weak, then I am strong* (2 Corinthians 12:10 NIV).

So you will go through difficulties, insults, hardships, heartaches, and bothers of the world, but God is giving you strength to overcome—depending on how you choose to go through those difficulties. Will you delight in them like Paul did? Will you be boastful or bitter?

Boastful or Bitter?

I speak to you as you sit in the difficulties, insults, hardships, and bothers of the world. I tell you that you will come out of this! You were born to be great, and God has not given up on you. If you can trust Him in your weakest place, He can grant you power. If you can look to God when it is all falling apart, then He can lift you up and put it all back together again. He said no to weaken you, and He weakened you so He could give you strength. It's hard and it's heavy, but when you lay your weaknesses out, God will strengthen you.

You may feel alone, but God is not a man that He should lie. If He said He's going to do it, then you just have to stand on the fact that He will. Sometimes we can hear a no and it can detour us and we start to doubt God, but we have come too far to give up now! You are walking in great purpose, and you have to stay the course. When we have decided to trust God above all, there will always be obstacles and mountains, and we have to be able to be strong enough to faith it through those obstacles. I know it's not easy, and I know you want to give up, and I know it's not fair, but God gave you the no so that you would let your power go, and replace it with His power.

I am reminded of a story I heard of a woman who birthed twins. One survived and the other was pronounced dead after several attempts to resuscitate the infant. The mother and father wanted to say good-bye to their son and decided to hold him. The mother instinctively laid her lifeless newborn baby across her breast and was saying good-bye when the baby began to move. The doctor was called in. He responded by saying that the baby is dead, and those are just normal reflexes. They continued to hold the child and they began to see his eyes open. She tried to feed her son a drop of breast milk from her finger, and her son took it with excitement, and even after that the doctor didn't believe her and her husband. The doctor told her there was nothing he could do, and they needed to accept that their son was dead. She kept holding him, and he kept getting life (power) with every moment. She embraced the weak and scary spots and did not become bitter, and her child began to get more life.

This mother was in her weakest moment with a little bit of faith, wisdom, and understanding,

He said no to weaken you, and He weakened you so He could give you strength.

and God turned her weakness into His power. Two hours later, after holding him, he began to get color in his face and he started breathing. The doctor came back and was astonished to find out that the baby was breathing, responding, and he had a heartbeat. You may be holding on to a dead thing, and hoping it will gain life, but if you would hold on and let God turn your weak area into your most powerful moment, you can bring life to a dead thing. Your promise is worth the no because there is power in the no.

You may be facing your hardest, weakest thing, but if you can just hold on and allow God to consume you with His power, you will overcome in this situation. You will rise above this thing and you will bring life to something that you thought was dead. You are empowered to succeed.

There is power in the no.

Though the storms in life are raging, know that there is peace in your ability to embrace God's strategy. I have heard several nos in life, and some have shaken me, but none of them have broken me. I have gone through pain in life, but I have found that God has remained my strength—as long as I was able to embrace my weaknesses. So stop running away from the difficulties of life. Stop asking God to take away your weak spots and embrace them instead. It's okay to be weak as long as you realize that God is strong.

Now His Power Rests on Me

Wait! Our Scripture ends with the promise that God's power will rest on us.

Therefore I will boast all the more gladly about my weaknesses, so that Christ's power may rest on me (2 Corinthians 12:9 NIV).

You can have access to power, but it just hasn't rested on you yet. What are you allowing to rest on you? You can have weaknesses, difficulties, and even insults, but don't become the weakness. Overcome the weaknesses by embracing your weakest points when everything is falling apart. Look to the hills from whence cometh your help and you will overcome that weakness and receive power.

So now, let me speak to you. It's time for you to begin to show God that you are a good investment. God has planted something in you, and it's time for you to produce it. Stop brushing your pain and difficulties under the rug and start showing your scars. You are brought to strength in your ability to show your scars.

I had a lot of scars and a lot of pain. I walked in blame, which just made me even weaker. There were boyfriends who said they loved me and physically abused me. Then I was raped by someone who told me he loved me. Now that's a weakness, and I was afraid of facing that scar. That scar is there, but I'm still standing.

I was afraid of trusting that scar with anyone, but here I am trusting it with you because I've found strength in my pain. I found strength in the God who stood with me while I endured the pain. He was orchestrating my victory over the violence. I tried it on my own, and I failed every time, but when I sought God I found Him, and when I knocked on the door He answered. God called me to the door, and I said yes.

You have been chosen for such a time as this, to be bigger than what you think. God has called you to the door, and what's behind this door is bigger than what you think you deserve. He will give you the power to obtain your purpose, and that purpose is something that this world needs. There are hills you have to climb, but you do not climb them alone. And you don't climb them without power—you have obtained your power in the strangest spot. You have something that needs to be produced, and I can't wait to see you produce it. God may have said no, and you may have felt weak, but guess what? There is power in the no!

Start showing your scars.

Your scars are not a symbol of embarrassment, they are a symbol of power. You overcame, you survived. Often I hear people upset about their bruises, scars, hurts, and pains and they don't want to show them. I think to myself, do you know how many people went through the same thing you went through, and they didn't make it? Do you know how many people lost their battle because they focused on hiding their weaknesses over gaining their power? Your scars are not embarrassing, they are necessary, purposeful, and powerful. Yes, our scars show our weaknesses, but they are beautiful to God. You will become mighty because of your scars. You will join a movement of world changers because of your scars.

Stop running from the pain and the bleedings, because that's what makes you beautiful and identifies you as a world changer. Guess what? There was a man carrying a cross to Calvary. They beat Him, they crushed Him, they pierced Him in the side, they nailed His hands and His feet, and they mocked His position as King. They laid Him in a tomb and on the third day He rose again with all power in His pierced, nailed, scarred hands.

The thing that makes Him the King of kings and the Lord of lords is His scars. Do not spend one more day covering up your scars. Your scars are the crown of His grace!

> *I pray right now that you would come out of the darkness into the light. I plead the blood of Jesus over every pain, over every scar, over every weakness, and I pray, God, that You bring strength right now to the forefront. I pray, God, right now that You deliver my friend and show them the beauty in their scars and the power in their weakness. I pray, God, that You would demolish the pain that they have carried and that You create in them a clean heart. Lord, wherever they are and whatever they are doing, meet them where they are and comfort them right now. Take away the hurt, anger, and loss, for You are God and God alone. You are great and You have all power.*
>
> *God, crown them with grace and fill them with Your fire right now in the name of*

The thing that makes Him the King of Kings and the Lord of Lords is His scars.

Jesus. Align them in the spirit realm that they walk in that alignment. Lord, I pray that You clean their surroundings and cleanse their thoughts of anything that is not matching with Your will for their life. I thank You, God, that You are bringing restoration in their family's life, and that You are bringing healing. In the name of Jesus, it is so. And so it is. Amen.

Scan this code for Cora's Chapter 8
PRAYER FOR YOU!

Or Visit
WWW.CORAJAKESCOLEMAN.COM

NINE

Considered Worthy for the Struggle

For everyone born of God overcomes the world.
This is the victory that has overcome
the world, even our faith.

(1 John 5:4 NIV)

You are going to change the world with what God put in you. The world needs your message and people need to hear what you overcame. You have not been forgotten. You have been hidden for a long time, and God is going to shine a light on whatever you decide to touch. Whatever you ask for from God will be given to you in this season and window. Stop worrying if you are good enough. Stop doubting yourself. Stop doubting your ability and believe in yourself. Come forth. It's time for you to be great.

The world will miss what you have to say and what you have to produce if you stay focused on the "why me?" and not on the rewards after the pain. The rainbow is promised to you after the storm. Noah didn't focus on the storm; he focused on looking for land. He was faithful to obey God and not worry, and after the flood God gave him the promise in the rainbow (see Genesis 9). Have you been concentrating on the flood? I'm here to tell you that God is going to give you the rainbow as soon as you stop looking at the flood. You are free from the wars of the world. Go forward in God's grace and peace.

Come forth. It's time for you to be great.

Your Story for the Next Generation

It's time to push this baby out, but your unbelief can abort heaven's destiny for your life. It's time for you to believe in God and it's time to believe in yourself. You have been implanted with a seed of purpose and power, and it will erupt in the cities and in the fields. The harvest that you produce will overflow for every generation that lived before you and every generation yet to come. You are the manifestation of the hope of God. God's hope for you is prosperous, and you will be mighty in your area and in your call.

You are God's book—a best seller! And you will produce powerful works for God. Don't faint! Don't quit! He is still performing miracles for His children. God has considered you worthy because there is a gem inside of you that God needs, and He wants to see it come forth.

I'm thrilled that God considered me and wrote my story. So far I've lived that story and overcame in that story. Yes, I am still waiting for my Nehemiah. I am standing on God's Word and on my purpose. My passion for Nehemiah will produce my purpose, and he will come forth. I don't know what God is considering you for, I just know that He's considering you. I know that your birthing is just around the corner. You may have to go through some fire and some crushing, but God has chosen you to go through the struggle so that you can speak about the success when you come out of it. Think about it. Job was considered worthy of this great struggle that produced purpose. Moses was considered, Esther was considered, David was considered, Daniel was considered, and Shadrach, Meshach, and Abednego were considered. All of these saints had to withstand the struggle, and all of them received power, success, and promotion—but not without the pain of the struggle and the birth of the promise.

Your portion is worth the pain and the struggle that it will take for you to get there. Your portion is worth the pain and hurt of the process. Your portion is worth the obstacles that tried to stand in your way.

You have all power. Your position is needed in the Kingdom. Take your seat and stay there, no matter what you have to go through. Understand that your life is a testament of what you were willing to overcome.

God did not consider any of the people I listed above to go through pain. God considered them for their portion. He considered them worthy to impact the next generation. God has a specific plan and strategy laid out for your life, and all you have to do is walk through the storm with your head held high, without hesitation, and let God know that "though He slay me, yet will I trust Him" (Job 13:15). You have been designed to have the victory—all you need to do is walk it out. Your rainbow, your double portion, your crown, and your promotion are on the way. You have been considered worthy for this struggle because God sees your success just ahead.

You Are an Overcomer!

You were born to overcome.

I never really understood my struggle until I saw ahead to the success that was coming and the reward behind it. When you are in the moment, it's hard to see what God is doing. It can be a lonely place where you are looking for answers in a room where there are no answers to find, and God's voice is ever so silent. But I have learned that when God is being quiet, He is working on my behalf. I used to get angry at God's voice, but I understood that God was just orchestrating my success and preparing my portion. I understand that my life is the Lord's, and with that understanding comes the acceptance that there are times when I need to be quiet and let Him speak.

You are a natural overcomer because you are a child of God.

> *For everyone born of God overcomes the world. This is the victory that has overcome the world, even our faith* (1 John 5:4 NIV).

You were born to overcome. Everyone born of God overcomes the world. So let me ask you this question: Are you born of God? Are you pretending or are you really faithing it? Do you really believe?

There are a lot of people who adhere to the idea and theory of God, go to church, pretend to know God, and pretend to be a Christian, but aren't truly dedicated and born of God. You must first be born of God to birth the new promise of God.

Worship Him in Spirit and in Truth

We each need to know our own heart. Be honest with ourselves. Jesus said that those who worship Him must worship Him in spirit and in truth (see John 4:23–24). What if I could tell that you have been born of God only by the way I look at your worship? Are you a pretender or are you practicing truth?

I can remember as a little girl seeing people worship around me in church services. Some would have tears in their eyes, others would be on their knees and crying out to God. I could actually feel the compassion in their hearts for God. When I was little, I wanted to know what that feeling was like. I wanted to have that kind of passion for God, and even though I was a little girl I went toward God because of what I saw in spirit and truth. We don't have examples like that very much in church anymore, but you have the ability to grasp it.

I reached toward God and allowed Him to consume me. I chose God, and in my choosing God He choose me, and I became born of God. When God became my Father, my guide, and my director, I naturally became an overcomer and the victory of the world was placed in my hand. You can be of the world and born of the world, but that position will never make you an overcomer of the world. If you want to overcome and find the power in the struggle, you have to say no to the world for yourself. This chapter isn't just about the fact that God considered you for the struggle, but it's about whether you are going to make the decision to consider God.

I want to encourage you to humble yourself before God and say, "God, You are my Father. I worship You in spirit and in truth. I delight myself in You. I am Yours and You are mine."

It's Our Choice

We are all placed in the world with the right to make a choice to choose God or to choose the world. When you place God at the forefront of your choices in life, then you are officially placed behind God where He protects you and the seed He has placed inside of you.

Why do we put up walls? We put up walls to protect ourselves from getting hurt. We go through life and we shut people out of the real pain and weight that we go through. We become so good at it that we shield ourselves from even God being able to penetrate that wall. So we give God a little, but we hold back the real weight, the real truth of our being. We can get very good at protecting ourselves. You have been hiding behind your wall for too long. Remember, there is nothing behind your wall that is too hard for God to handle.

God can only be before you if you choose Him to be in that place—at the forefront of your life. When you are considered by God, you are considered for the struggle, just like Job. The hedge of protection around you is compromised when God considers you. Suddenly you find that you are tested and tried because God needs to at this point find out if you are really for Him. God needs to know if you really believe that He is for you. God needs to know if you will worship Him over your worry. If you are born of Him, you will overcome in your struggle.

Loved in Spite of Our Imperfections

I know you have lived a life with rejection, and you wanted someone to believe in you, and you needed someone to support you and walk with you, and every time you let someone behind your wall they would hurt you and take a piece of you with them. I know that you have spent nights crying for someone to love and accept you even with your flaws and imperfections. I know you're waiting for someone to see you as the person that you really want to be, and you want them to be okay with it. I know you've felt misunderstood and perhaps even felt dead looking for life.

It's time to trust God with all of that rejection. Bring the heartbreak, the pain, the sorrow, the shame, the humiliation, the devastation, the depression, the suicidal thoughts, the doubts, and the worry, and lay it all down before God. Break yourself for God's glory. God was crushed and beaten and humiliated for you. He did it all just for you.

He died for the purpose and the beauty that is in you.

He died for the things you are too afraid and embarrassed to show.

He died for the lost.

He died for the hungry.

He died for the sick and the hurting.

He died for all of that because He saw *you* worth considering. He saw what God had planned for you. He saw the power in your ability to give Him your pain.

You have been looking for someone to accept and consider you. Well, God says, "I have considered you. I have loved you. I have loved you without your mask. I have loved you while you were writing your suicide note, and that's why it didn't work—because I loved you in your weakness. I loved you when he or she left you. I loved you when you were alone. I loved you when you didn't love yourself. I loved you when you wouldn't dare take a picture. I loved you when I took your brother. I loved you when you lost your baby. I loved you when you buried your mother and your father. I loved you. I considered you. I love you and I just want you to pick Me—let me behind that wall of anger." God says, "I love you now even while you are angry with Me. I loved you when you are cursing your life because of the consideration of the struggle I am bringing you through. I love you."

It's hard to feel love when you are in so much pain, but God does love you. He loved you so much that He gave His only Son—not one of His sons, His *only* Son. And whoever believes in Him will not perish in his struggle (see John 3:16).

You will not perish in the storm.

You will not perish with the backlash.

You will not perish in humiliation.

You will not perish in abandonment.

You will not perish in rejection.

God gave us Jesus so that we will have everlasting life. God gave His Son's life for your life. It may not seem like it, and you may not feel like it, but He did. You have been considered just as Jesus was considered. You are royalty and you will get to your crown, but you must allow God to break down that wall you've put up so that He can build His purpose in you.

You have a legacy to fulfill and to leave behind. You are considered for a blessing of supernatural portions. You were created to birth the promise of God. You have no reason to be afraid. Do not be afraid for God is with you. Expect that now that you have accepted God as your Father, the enemy is going to come after you. Don't fight it, resist it and strengthen your faith. Stay close to God and continue to worship in spite of what you may be going through. God's got you. God is your Father now and that is different from accepting Him as your Savior. When you make God your Father, you are giving Him access to every part of you that is both pleasing and unpleasing to yourself. You are deciding to trust Him to direct, to discipline, to lead, to guide, and to love you unconditionally. You are entering into a relationship with God where He is not an outer entity—He is both an outer orchestrator of your life and inner orchestrator of your being.

Here is something for you to pray every day:

God, You are my Father. I am an open vessel willing to serve You however You would have me to. Give me the strength to walk through what You have considered me to accomplish today. God give me the strength to withstand the enemy's attacks. Protect, lead, and guide me according to Your perfect will, and I will be forever grateful. Amen.

You may not have it all together, and you may still need some help, but guess what? We aren't finished yet. We are still walking this journey together. We are still faithing it together. I promise you that the best is yet to come.

God in the Birthing Room— PUSH!

Here's the question: Are you willing to push aside what people may say so that you can encounter God and gain His power? Are you willing to gain your heart's desires no matter what that means? Are you ready to make that sacrifice to press through, or will you settle for mediocre desires, mediocre life, with mediocre purpose? We cannot let what people say keep us from our encounter.

Without our own new birth, we don't receive the power.

Without the power, we can't obtain wholeness.

Without wholeness, we cannot birth God's promise.

Your success comes in your ability to surrender yourself to satisfy God so that He can consume the very essence of your being. Even if the road is bumpy, even if they are talking about you, even if they never understood you, and even if you don't understand yourself, you stay strong. In the middle of your doubt, reach for God with an ounce of faith and He will grant you His power.

The woman with the issue of blood fought through the crowd while she was bleeding, stinking, fragile, weak, humiliated, embarrassed, and passed the people who ridiculed her. She crawled through that crowd with just a little bit of faith that if she touched the hem of His garment she would be made whole. Your power comes when your reach for that hem. But your wholeness comes in your encounter with God.

Although she was afraid of what would happen, the woman with the issue of blood pressed through to encounter God, and because of this He made her whole. Some of you have allowed your humiliation, your embarrassment, and your "judgers" to keep you from your encounter. It is not until you allow yourself to walk past what people will say that you can encounter God and be made whole. Your healing and wholeness comes from your passion to encounter God.

You deserve to have your heart's desires, but God also deserves that you delight yourself in Him. Have you surrounded yourself with righteousness? Then prepare yourself now to let go of your past, failures, mistakes, hurts, angers, and losses. Don't allow yourself to be consumed by your past! Don't focus on the things you can't change. Instead, go after the thing that God wants. You must want more for yourself than to live your life in the bitterness of the past. Bitterness will produce a dead thing because you have self-sabotaged and committed intoxication of the soul, mind, and body. Don't go there.

Your power comes when your reach for that hem.

I challenge you to look beyond yourself so that you can birth your dream and grab hold of what truly matters. You deserve to know that there is nothing you can do about the past except walk past it. Ask God to heal you by faith, and desire more for yourself so that when you have your encounter with Christ you are able to gain power and wholeness.

It's important for me to let you know that you are better than this, and you deserve what God has planted inside of you. Don't let yourself be consumed by distractions. Just because it happens doesn't mean that God meant you to have it and to focus on it. The enemy will present a distraction every time you are about to walk into your purpose because it is a threat to his kingdom. Don't get distracted. Allow yourself the opportunity to be bigger, better, and greater than your distractions.

And don't assume that because you are personally discouraged with yourself that God is discouraged with you. God is not discouraged with you. God is delivering you!

Delivery Is COMING!

I am reminded of when my godsister went into labor with my godson. She was in pain the whole time, until she pushed my godson out. When God plants something in you, it's bigger than you! It's bigger than your comprehension! It's God's seed planted in you—a seed called purpose—and you have to reach for it. With every delivery there will be a process, pain, embarrassment, unbearable laboring, heavy breathing, highs and lows, changes of breath, people in your business, a lot of surroundings, detachment, and nurturing.

You are supposed to birth your purpose.

You are supposed be stretched.

You are supposed to be in pain.

If you concentrate more on the pain, then when it's time for you to birth (just like a real labor) you will be too tired, and you will feel like you can't do it. Some people push longer than others. Some people hurt more than others. The point is that they are all birthing! And God shows us in the birthing process that beauty can come from a painful thing.

There is beauty in your pain. Maybe you just haven't pushed it out yet, and you're still faithing for it, but keep faithing because if you don't you won't birth. Don't get stuck! Some of us stay stuck in the pain so we aren't able to birth and we aren't able to nurture because we have allowed ourselves to become consumed by the pain.

Meanwhile, your purpose (your baby) is waiting until you push. It's going to stretch you. It's supposed to hurt. Do not give up! PUSH!

Beauty can come from a painful thing.

PUSH!

I am your birthing coach and I am telling you, "Breathe!" Don't give up, it's time to start faithing. Allow it to happen, and *push* this thing out.

When they are in your business, push it out.

When people don't agree, push it out.

Deliver through the pain.

When you are all alone and tired to the bone, push it out.

It's time to rise! You deserve to rise. You deserve to come forth—you deserve to have your promise in your hand. You have to be willing to have an encounter in order to birth.

You don't get to the greatest part of having a baby until you have gone through the pain. After that long stretch of pain, you hold your beautiful newborn in your arms. When God places something in you, there are steps just like in a pregnancy. Once you identify you are pregnant, you must seek good counsel. You must follow instructions to keep the baby and the birth as healthy as possible.

If you are fighting and laboring, tired and weary, then you are in the process and that just means you are that much closer to your promise! The road is going to be hard, but in the end it will be worth it. Your destination to your desires lie in your ability to allow yourself to deliver through the pain. Fight the good fight of faith!

I realize that you can grow tired of fighting, but if you give up the fight then God will pass your purpose to someone else. Expect that the enemy is going to attack your purpose.

You are aligned with God.

You are connected with God.

You are in the lineage of royalty!

Anything that comes through you is stronger than what you could have thought of because you have connected yourself with Christ. Whatever you walk in is more powerful than you could imagine. If you truly walked in the full capacity of what God had for you and what you have access to, then you would change the nation. Make a decision to understand that you are royalty.

Your biggest success comes after your biggest sacrifice.

My challenge to you here is to work on learning about yourself so that you can recognize your value. If you believe in yourself as much as God believes in you, then you will walk in a confidence that is even more of a threat to the enemy.

God is not through with you—He is just getting started with you! Your delight is connected to your desires and you have the power. You deserve to pursue your purpose, and when you are ready to walk into your true purpose God will make a way, and He will make the crooked path straight for you. Your biggest success comes after your biggest sacrifice.

Hands Off the Windows!

My biggest sacrifice was my own will. I was so passionate about my heart's desire that I took over instead of letting God take over. I didn't allow God to consume me. Instead, I made myself God to everyone around me, and admittedly I had to deliver myself from pride and arrogance, thinking that I could do a better job than God could. I had to say, "Okay, I let go and let God."

When I surrendered and sacrificed myself and my will, it was very scary for me. But I did it to better myself. I was finally able to sacrifice everything I ever wanted and submit to the fact that whatever God gives me is bigger than anything I could ever desire.

When I took my hands off the windows, He was able to open the windows and pour me out a blessing I did not have room enough to receive.

> *"Try Me now in this," says the Lord of hosts, "if I will not open for you the **windows** of heaven and pour out for you such blessing that there will not be room enough to receive it"* (Malachi 3:10).

We have to move our hands off the windows so that God can open, and then and only then will we be able to receive what He pours out. When I took my hands off the windows and allowed God to orchestrate my blessings, that's when I was blessed with my daughter, my calling, and many other things.

Every day I am sacrificing myself to what God would have for me. Every day I am emptying myself of myself. Because of my ability to trust that God's thoughts are indeed higher than mine, I am able to say, "God, help me to see me the way You see me." At that point I am submitting my thoughts to what God thinks.

I let my thoughts center around what God sees. I allow myself, my life, and my story to be an open vessel for Him to write my story for me. If you allow God to write for you, when you allow Him to become a piece of you, then He directs and orders your steps.

Because of my submission, I know and believe that soon I will be writing about how God blessed me with birthing a son.

What do you believe God for? Are you holding on to the window? Are you ready to let go? Are you ready to let Him open it and pour out your blessings?

Or are you scared to trust Him because you are being consumed by past pains and hurts that He made you walk though in your process?

Come forward, dear heart, the nation needs you! It's time for you to let go of the hurts of your past, and begin to live in your process and reach for the hem of His garment. You're wanted in the birthing room. PUSH!

God in heaven, You are the Creator of all things and You have created something beautiful for my friend to receive. You have created something beautiful for them to birth. I pray, God, that You will leap them into their double portion. I pray, God, that You leap them into their rightful place and position in the Kingdom. God, I pray that You would give them a forgiving heart and that they be a forgiver to those who have harmed, hurt, and misunderstood them. I pray, God, You mend the broken relationships that You brought together and tear apart the ones You didn't.

Lord, I pray You instill them with passion for their purpose and remove their passion for pain. I rebuke every suicidal thought, every spirit of depression, everything that is not like You. I bind it up and send it back to the pit of hell from which it came. God, You control the order of their steps, so order them accordingly.

I thank You, God, for placing a crown on Your child's head and showing them that they have been considered by a man who has a double portion waiting for them. God, I thank

You for rebirthing them into You, for we know that if they are born of God they are overcomers. Thank You, God, for I believe it is done, and it is so and so it is in the name of Jesus. Amen.

God, I thank You that You are making a way where there seems to be no way, and God, I pray for a supernatural healing for my friend from the inside out. Every ailment, every problem, every curse that has tried to attach itself to this reader, we call it broken by the power of the Holy Ghost. You are God and God alone, and before time began You were on Your throne.

Lord, I thank You that You have considered them for the struggle, but that they are about to birth their promise. I thank You, God, that all things work together for the good of those who have been called according to Your purpose and will for their lives. We trust You for the divine timing and order of all these things, in Jesus' name. Amen and amen.

Scan this code for Cora's Chapter 9
PRAYER FOR YOU!

Or Visit
WWW.CORAJAKESCOLEMAN.COM

CHAPTER TEN

Covenant Relationship

Fight the good fight of the faith. Take hold
of the eternal life to which you were called
when you made your good confession
in the presence of many witnesses.

(1 TIMOTHY 6:12 NIV)

You've been considered worthy by God to birth His dreams for your life and for the next generation. You are being trained for the fight by the best coach in the world—get ready! It's time to get into the ring. Every good boxer has to prepare for the fight, and God wants to prepare us in the same way. We are in a faith fight, and there is more to faith than just saying you have it. You have to be ready for the fight. You can get caught up looking to use what has worked for everyone else, but you need to use what works for you.

You can run into the ring impulsively, but I warn you to plan first. Everyone has a fight to fight, and their winning is specific to strategy. Be careful what you choose to fight with. You want to make sure that you face the giants in your life with no fear, full preparation, a good strategy, and most importantly, your coach.

When I was diagnosed with infertility, I had to go through IVF. When it failed in the first cycle, I went to God in devastation and heartbreak and said, "God, if You are going to make me go through this, You'd better make it count." At that time I also began to write to my promise (Nehemiah), and I told my promise, "I will fight for you...." Then I began to research to look up and find information. I sought good counsel and wisdom and understanding so that I could win.

It's time to get into the ring.

You will get the victory with God, but your faith must rest on substance. Hebrews 11:1 says, "Now faith is the substance of things hoped for, the evidence of things not seen."

If you have no substance, then you are only halfway in. You can't fight Goliath without a sling and stones. You can't fight your battle without substance—your wisdom and your weapon. Once you have everything in your hand, then you may get in the ring. I got in the ring with my faith, my coach, my wisdom, my understanding, and my armor, and I believed God for the impossible because I know with Him all things are possible.

I know that you have been ignited and you are ready to take on the world, but it is wise to get understanding and seek counsel before you take on your giant. You have to put on the correct armor that fits you. More importantly, you need to submit your fight to the power that God has already placed in your hand. No one ever won a battle without studying, practicing, and seeking counsel.

Know Your God

Now that you have been ignited for the fight, it's time for you to gain knowledge. Get in the Word of God and find out about what you are fighting so that when the giant rises you don't lose. I was thinking the other day about how much Word I have in me. Then I wondered about something. If I was only able to fight the enemy based on the Word that I have in my heart, would I win or lose? You can have God behind you and be consumed by God, but do you know about the God who is in you? Have you searched His Word? Do you know His capability? Do you have an understanding of just how powerful you are when you're consumed by Him?

Before you fight for the promise in God's hand, before you fight for the purpose that God has for you, before you step into the ring with the giants of the world, *know your God.* Know about Him, what He went through, and what He thinks of you. Trust me, you won't be able to know everything, but show God that this isn't a one-way street where you have become close to Him because you want to gain something from Him.

Show God your motives in this relationship. Tell Him that you want to think about Him more and more, and that you want to know Him personally. You need to become of God so that He can become of you, and you can become one. Your heart should be so into God that the people who want to be around you have to seek God in order to find you!

Stand Up for God

As Christians in the Kingdom, we have to take a stand for God. The media will shut us down, the radio won't want to hear from us. It's easier to conform to the world than change it. God is calling the anointed leaders of this generation to come forth.

Isaiahs, come forth.

Malachis, come forth.

Obadiahs, come forth.

Nehemiahs, come forth.

Esthers, come forth.

Marys, come forth.

Someone needs to speak up for God. We can spend so much time wanting God to stand up for us, but He needs us to stand up for Him too! We are Kingdom kids and it's time we start acting like it. If we don't make God's voice known, then His voice and His movement will die. He will be condemned again, and His crucifixion will mean nothing.

He died for us. At the very least we can stand up for Him. Yes, this is what it's about. We stand for Him because when we take on this giant Goliath, we are going to have to be able to say that God

It's easier to conform to the world than change it.

and I are standing together. It is pointless to say that God is for you if you aren't for Him. Your relationship with God requires a level of responsibility. If you are unwilling to take responsibility in the world and in the spirit realm, then you will lose. You can stand for God and pretend, but the reality is if you deny Him in any element of your life, you will not be able to produce the power that is rightfully yours through relationship.

Can you stand for God in places where it's hard to stand? Are you willing to stand for Christ in public and in private? Is your relationship status with God complicated? Are you a God gold digger always seeking for what He can give you and unwilling to give back, or even say thank You?

Champions become champions based on the relationship and understanding that they have with the coach. A champion cannot win if he or she has a complicated, unyielding, rebellious relationship with the coach.

Check Your Relationship Status

So here comes your next challenge: Check yourself and your relationship with God. You are almost there. You are about to face your giant, but in order to win, you need a strong relationship with your coach.

It's all about relationship. Why? In order to produce, nurture, and nourish a seed, there has to be some type of relationship with the seed and the producer. You cannot produce a seed without a connection.

Production starts with a connection. You must get connected to God in order to produce and birth what He planted. When you are filled with the Holy Spirit, you are filled with a seed, with life. And it all started with your ability to allow God to connect with you and to fill you. Now you have to stay connected so that you can bring forth what He placed inside you, much like a baby. Just like a baby. You are connected with that child forever. You will always be that child's mother or father. If you aren't producing, you must ask yourself, are you connected?

Sometimes we get upset because we aren't seeing our fruit and we aren't seeing our promise, but we have to check ourselves. Have we become God gold diggers? Are we consumed with ourselves and with asking God for the things we want? Is our hand always out, ready to take, but not to give?

Put yourself in position to be a giver and a receiver.

You'll never be able to give more to God than He could give to you, but you must at least put yourself in position to be a giver and a receiver. For it is indeed better to give than to receive. If you give to God and you mean it beyond your own personal gain, and give in a pure heart, then He will give back to you.

When I started giving to God, that is when I started receiving from God. We need to stop looking for materialistic things all the time. Sometimes a day of peace is what God gives to you. Sometimes that calm in the middle of the day brought through a phone call is what God gives to you. Whatever God gives, be grateful because it is all connected back to the Word. If you are faithful over the few things, God will make you ruler over many things. The roads to promise and purpose are not easy, but when I am connected to God in spirit and in truth, I can't lose. How do I know? Well, I am glad you asked.

Covenant Keeping God

One morning on a very hot day there stood a man over nine feet tall who tormented the Israelites and tried to start a war. He stood before the Israelites and challenged them to fight. First Samuel 17 tells us the story:

> *Choose a man for yourselves, and let him come down to me. If he is able to fight with me and kill me, then we will be your servants; but if I prevail against him and kill him, then you shall be our servants and serve us* (1 Samuel 17:8-9 WEB).

This nine-foot giant was named Goliath. He was large, loud, and obnoxious. Day after day Goliath came out and stood on the other side of the mountain and called to Israel. Goliath went so far as to defy God's army!

> *The Philistine said, "I defy the armies of Israel this day; give me a man, that we may fight together." When Saul and all Israel heard these words of the Philistine, they were dismayed, and greatly afraid* (1 Samuel 17:10 WEB).

The king of Israel, King Saul, and all of his armies were afraid of Goliath. He terrified all the Israelites—except one. There was a shepherd boy whose heart was for God. David was in a covenant relationship with God, and God gave him great power because of this. David's father asked him to leave his sheep to go see how his brothers were doing on the battlefield and to bring them some food from home.

David was just a teenager at the time, but when he heard Goliath shouting, he got angry. Why? Goliath had defied the living God. David said, "Who is this uncircumcised Philistine, that he should defy the armies of the living God?" (1 Samuel 17:26 WEB).

Circumcision was *the* sign of covenant with God in the Old Testament. All Hebrew baby boys were circumcised as a sign of the covenant between God and Israel. So when David said, "Who is this uncircumcised Philistine to defy the armies of the living God," David was pointing to the covenant God made with His people. David was saying, "This giant is big but he doesn't have a covenant with God—and God is bigger."

This giant is big but he doesn't have a covenant with God.

David stood for the living God because God had stood for him as a shepherd of sheep alone in the fields, and God hadn't failed him. David knew that God helped him defeat a lion and a bear as he watched sheep in the fields, and he was utterly confident that God would help him defeat this giant too. What I love about the story the most is that David didn't take credit for defeating the lion and the bear; rather, he gave the credit to God. We often get so locked up in trying to take credit for a battle that we couldn't even overcome if it hadn't been for the Lord. Give God the credit for the fight He helped you win before you got in the ring. You will defeat this new Goliath. So right now before I even continue, I want you to think of everything you overcame and thank God and give Him the honor for it.

David went before this giant with five smooth rocks and a sling in his hand. I love what David shouted back at Goliath. Just listen to the war cry of this shepherd boy:

> *Then David said to the Philistine, "You come to me with a sword, with a spear, and with a javelin. But I come to you in the name of the Lord of hosts, the God of the armies of Israel, whom you have defied. This day the Lord will deliver you into my hand, and I will strike you and take your head from you. And this day I will give the carcasses of the camp of the Philistines to the birds of the air and the wild beasts of the earth, that all the earth may know that there is a God in Israel. Then all this assembly shall know that the Lord does not save with sword and spear; for the battle is the Lord's, and He will give you into our hands"* (1 Samuel 17:45–47).

And you know the rest of the story. David defeated Goliath that day. When we are born again, we enter into a covenant with God through the shed blood of Jesus Christ. When you are in covenant with God and you respect the position and the "bigness" of God, you face your giant fully equipped. You don't need anything but the Lord God Almighty.

For years David sang to God all alone in the fields as he watched the sheep. For years he had declared his desire and delighted himself in the Lord. In fact, David wrote that verse in the book of Psalms: "Delight yourself also in the Lord, and He shall give you the desires of your heart" (37:4). David stood for God and showed both the believers and the nonbelievers that there was a God.

So I ask you, what have you charged your giant with? Have you charged your giant with God beside you or God consuming you? Do you realize you are in covenant with God?

Time to Know God and Refuse Fear

Here's our second challenge in this chapter: How much time do you spend getting to know God and really consuming yourself with His Word and communicating with Him? If you spend more time on Facebook than you do fasting and talking to God, then when you are faced with your giant you won't win. Do you know more about your stats on your social media then you do about Scriptures? Come on now!

You can't expect success without the knowledge of the Scriptures of God. You must get to know God in order for Him to use you as an open vessel, and when you are an open vessel for Him, then He stands before you. He fights the battle for you and you are named victorious because He claimed the victory for you. You aren't victorious, the God in you that you choose to gain knowledge of is victorious. You aren't to be a God gold digger anymore. I teach my children in Destiny World that we must learn to say thank you to God before we dare open our mouth to say please.

Don't be someone who only opens your Bible at church or Bible study or when bad things are going on. Don't be someone who prays only when you want something or need God to get you out of something. Don't be the type of person who only praises God on Sunday and choir rehearsal, but let praise continuously be in your mouth. Seek the Lord daily. Read His Word daily and hide it (memorize it) in your heart. Like David, you are a winner when you attach yourself to God and to the Word of God. Remember,

God is older, wiser, and much bigger than any old giant that comes your way. Trust Him! He's the greatest and wisest coach in the world.

When my daughter was a little girl, she was afraid of monsters *in* her bed, *under* her bed, and around her room. After a few nights with us, she came running in the room to tell me and my husband that there was a monster in her room. I told her to go into her room and to pray and say, "Jesus." But before I said any of that, I told her that monsters aren't real. To her they were real, but the minute that someone more powerful, older, and wiser told her that they weren't real she believed it, and she isn't afraid of monsters anymore. She laughs now when she hears kids say they are afraid of monsters.

Learn to say thank you to God before we dare open our mouth to say please.

Why did I tell you this? It's simple. If someone more powerful, wiser, and stronger didn't tell her that monsters weren't real, she would still be afraid of the monster. God is more powerful, wiser, and stronger than you. You may be faced with what looks like a monster, but God says it's not real. You are seeing the flood coming, but it's not going to drown you, and He has built a standard against it. You are seeing the weapon form, but it won't prosper. God says, "Your enemy, this monster, is nothing. I am bigger and stronger and more powerful than he will ever be. Now pray and go to sleep, sweetheart, and believe that I have you."

When you have the word of someone more powerful and stronger than you, then you rest in that. You can rest with God and know that He will face your giant with you, for you, and within you. God wants to give you your power, love, and your self-discipline—you just need to let your fear go. The hardest part of a relationship is taking that risk of getting hurt and not recovering.

God wants you to take a risk on Him. Choose Him now. Really choose Him in all things and in every element of your life so that He can take control and work His power through you. You are almost there to the promise—it's right there. You will achieve, you just have to get to know God so that He can be of you.

I gave the Lord my heart and asked for His. I allowed Him to have access to me at all times every day. God produces beauty from my broken pieces and I want to be connected to that kind of flow. I want to be a light in the darkness of this world. In order for me to be a light, I must submit and let God consume me with the light that is Him.

Love God, Not Religion

It's easy to get stuck in religion and the rules of religion. God did not come for religion, He came for relationship. He came for love. To put God's relationship in the rules of religion is wrong because that's not what He came for. A part of the relationship challenge is that you loose yourself from religious rules and get connected to the relationship with God. That's what attracted me to God—not religion but the relationship that I saw He had with others. Religion can push people away, but God's love draws a crowd.

You can love God and not love religion. God wants your heart, not your long skirt or your nail polish or your tattoos or your cleavage or your panty hose or your makeup or your contacts. God came so that you would give your heart and soul to Him and that you would develop a love for Him that He had for you. He wants to show you His heart toward you, and in return you allow God to connect with you on an emotional level. He is your friend.

We are designed to have and pursue relationships. We need to make sure that the relationship with God is firm before we search for relationship with others. Make sure that you are having as many intimate moments with God as you are having dates and agendas with people. If you truly love God and you are spending time with Him above all others, then you are faithing it!

God's love draws a crowd.

So guess what? Your faithing is in your hands now. Your promise is in your hands now, and all you have to do is speak to it. Everything you need is already in your hands. You have the victory. There is nothing left to do. Take hold, walk forward, for you are headed into covenant with Christ. God bless you and soar on!

Single-Hearted Love

Let me take a moment now to speak to my single friends. If you are single, that's even better because you have access and more time than anyone else to develop a relationship with God that is true, dedicated, and real. Don't see your single life as a horrible fate, but enjoy this time together when you can have undistracted devotion to God. God loves you so much and needs you to fall more in love with Him, and He is giving you the time to do so.

Another wonderful thing about this is that when you allow God to be everything to you and the right person does come along, your relationship will be so tight in God that He will be able to tell you what's for you and what's not for you.

This is hard, but I'm going to say it. Don't fight for a relationship that God didn't ordain. Let go of it—God has something better for you. Stop feeling like you have a responsibility to hold on to every relationship for whatever reason. God severs those ties for a reason, and you don't have to hold on to it. Let it go. God is for you, so trust Him to lead you to the right person.

If you are tied in a relationship that has become a dysfunction, a disease, a hardship, or an unbearable and painful situation for you, let it go. God is for you. He is for your heart, and when you have a solid relationship with God, the people around you will love you the way that God would have you to be loved.

God is orchestrating everything for your benefit. When you seek Him, He will give you the answers and put everything in order. Clean up your heart so that you can rightfully receive the heart of God and see people for who they really are. When you force yourself onto someone who is trying to show you they don't want you, then you are raping yourself. Not only that, you are preventing someone else from the person that God is trying to give to them. Don't rape yourself and don't rape anyone else. Walk away before you become a poison to the people who are supposed to gain from your purpose.

It's hard to let go of someone when you have let them love you, be intimate with you, and you have given them more of your heart than you have even given to God, but understand destruction comes in a relationship when you love man more than you have shown love to God. You cannot expect your relationship that was planted in sin, rooted in sin, and guided by sin to work.

There will always be someone who doesn't agree with the decisions you make to go toward Christ, but if Christ is in your heart you need not worry or be concerned because He will fix the discords and the distractions. God loves you. Sometimes you have to let go of the damage in order for God to pull you out of a dead place. If you keep playing with damaged goods, then you won't be able to gain access to God's power, purpose, and promise for your life. You need high-quality love in order to receive a high-quality promise.

Your relationship with God is your most powerful weapon.

It's important that you understand that your relationship with God is your most powerful weapon. Whatever you are going through, your fight is God's fight.

Do you want the covenant relationships you're involved in to be right before God? Do you want to sever the relationships that God did not ordain and nurture the relationships that are of Him? Let me pray for you now.

I pray that God will instill you with the

right people in your surroundings. You are no longer bound by dead relationships. You are loosed! I pray that God will connect you to people who are for you. I pray that God would remove you from dead situations and give you the strength to let go of the things He needs you to let go of. I pray that God would make you great before the people of God and that your relationship with Him would become a natural and consistent routine. I pray that God gives you the wisdom and the words to release the relationships that are not meant for you. I pray that you have the strength to walk away and you do not look back.

I pray that you be healed from the soul ties of the enemy and that you rebuild a foundation of God's truth. I pray that He strengthens the relationships that He brought together, and that He releases the relationships that He didn't bring together.

More importantly, I pray God's peace would consume every relationship the enemy is trying to shake up. I pray supernatural miracles to come forth in every relationship that is under the umbrella of God's choice and divine connection.

I pray that anything that is in you that would cause your God-ordained relationships to sever, that God would remove that thing and make you the glue that holds you and your loved ones together. May you have the faith and strength to stand for God above all things, and may God open doors for you according to your obedience and diligence toward Him. And it is so and so it is, in the mighty name of Jesus. Amen!

Scan this code for Cora's Chapter 10
PRAYER FOR YOU!

Or Visit
WWW.CORAJAKESCOLEMAN.COM

ELEVEN

Power Over Pride

What good is it for someone to gain the whole world,
and yet lose or forfeit their very self?

(LUKE 9:25 NIV)

You have a covenant with God Almighty and He has coached you and shown you how to faith it right into your promise. Victory is sweet, but you must know that when we get to the place of purpose that was promised to us, the enemy is going to come at us more now than he ever did before. God has given you the keys to the mansion—don't lose those keys because you aren't comfortable in your new position. Worse, don't lose those keys because you're *proud* of your new position. If the enemy can't get you tempted one way, he'll tempt you the other. He will try to make you feel uncomfortable in your placement and your position—a distraction you can't afford right now. If that doesn't work, he will feed your thoughts with how great you are and how there is no one like you.

What do you do? Keep your head held high and walk in this new place with a humble heart. Didn't God tell you He would bring you before great men and women? You are supposed to be here, so don't worry about what you have or don't have in the spirit realm. The truth is, you wear a victor's crown. You are now walking in faith like never before. You have been ignited, and you have fresh fire, and fresh perspective. All you need to do is keep ahold of this gift and don't lose yourself in yourself. You can't manage the gift of a mansion if your mindset is still in the projects or your old low-income apartment complex. And you will fall quickly if you think you are suddenly the best thing since sliced cheese. The Word of God tells us that pride goes before a fall. Stay humble.

Walk in this new place with a humble heart.

Don't Lose Ground

The good news is that when you are faced with these temptations or other tests, you are not alone. You have rekindled your relationship with God in spite of your pain, hurt, and anger. You have been held captive for some time, but God has not only unlocked you, He has given you the master key. As you go through the continued journey of faithing it, I urge you to stay close to God. Don't lose what you have gained in trusting and believing God. Do not lose the heart that you have toward Him. I urge you to stay focused on the blessings, not the bruises from the enemy. It's easy to lose the ground you've gained if you allow yourself to focus more on the battle and less on the blessing.

There is nothing left to fear and nothing to be bitter about now that God has orchestrated your purpose through this pain. You are going to be okay. You will go through battles, but you are not battling alone. Your purpose has made you productive. Your promise is beautiful and manifesting through your command.

Guard your faith just as David did. Do not let anyone sway you or allow your distractions and detours to control you. Control your distractions; do not submit to them. If you allow your mountains to destroy you or distract you, then you will easily lose your power. If the enemy comes to steal, kill, and destroy, then he has to do something that makes it easy for him to complete his assignment. The easiest way for him to do this is to bring forth a distraction. A distraction will make it easy for him to take the power out of your hand. If you get distracted, you'll be destroyed. Don't lose your power by taking the detours of life. Don't walk through every door in front of you because, as my mentor says, "Every door is not a God door."

Stay focused on the blessings, not the bruises from the enemy.

The Distraction of Looking Back

You may stand on high platforms and speak about your testimony, but none of it will matter if you aren't moving forward. You can sound deep and you can sound powerful, but if you let the devil steal your anointing, then you will not be able to destroy the attacks that come.

You have a decision to make, just as Lot's wife did. You can choose to walk toward your promise or you can look back to see what you just left behind and be paralyzed into a pillar of salt (see Genesis 19). And that was the end of her purpose and even her life. She was destroyed along with the stuff behind her. If you spend too much time looking at the stuff burning up behind you, then you will not accomplish the assignments in front of you. I want you to know that you have been given a unique gift from God. Don't worry about the cost it took for you to get it, because you will never know the cost it took for God to give you the gift of His Son.

When God takes you to a new level in life, He changes your position, your name, and your title. You are royalty! You own the light, and if you learn to walk in that mindset, everyone else will follow. You are a leader and you have been placed in the front of the line because God felt like you could lead people. You can wait for the world to tell you you're ready or you can tell the world to get ready. You have gone through a transformation. Yes, it has been heavy, but you have come out, and God has given you a crown on your head and a scepter of power in your hand. You have been deemed a daughter or son of the Most High, so walk like royalty. Don't get distracted or you will lose your position.

Don't Lose Yourself

Now let's talk about the power in your identity. Luke 9:25 says, "What good is it for someone to gain the whole world, and yet lose or forfeit their very self?" (NIV). God has called you great and placed you in position, but it's important that you remain humble. One form of pride is trying to fit in with everyone else. If you try to pray like someone else, speak like someone else, laugh like someone else, then you are losing your personal identity in order to identify with someone you admire. Do not lose yourself and who you are by trying to fit in with everyone else.

If you have yielded yourself to God through the process, stood up for God, let Him heal you, and you are walking in intimacy with Him, then your old mindset is gone. You aren't in the same mindset that you used to be. God has taken you to a new level, and not only do you personally see things differently, but the people around you will see *you* differently. That's a good thing. But let humility be your new identity. You walk with a different power now, but stay humble, solid, and don't lose yourself after all you have gained.

Walk like royalty.

I know that I have power to achieve greatness, but that has nothing to do with me, and it has everything to do with whom I am connected to. Don't become arrogant in your access. This access and authority comes through your submission to God, whereby you allow Him to control everything. We don't deserve it, but He uses us anyway.

Walk Like Royalty in Your New Level

We can easily let our power become arrogance in the Kingdom of God, where we feel entitled to our position. But God has not called you there because you are entitled, He put you there because what He put inside of you deserves to be in a great position. It is a humble person in royalty who continues to get promoted and get blessings in the Kingdom. Your obedience makes God want to grant you the promises. Lot obeyed what God said, and he made it to the promise. Moses hit the rock in anger, and he wasn't obedient, so he didn't gain his promise. He was not able to obtain the riches of the world in its fullness because he wasn't obedient. Your obedience is truly better than whatever you could sacrifice, because in your obedience God works for you.

So here is your challenge in this chapter: I challenge you to stay humble even when it's hard—even when you are provoked. I challenge you to answer the distractions of the enemy with prayer and obedience. Be led by God in all things. If you are faced with a distraction, answer that distraction with a move of God. If God says don't respond, don't respond and don't worry about whether they are going to be taken care of. God will protect you and fight for you. Don't lose yourself because of the mindset of others.

You have a new mindset, a new position, a new name, and it's time for you to stop looking behind you at the stuff God is destroying and start looking forward so that you can continue to obtain the promises of the land. God has opened the door. Don't look back! Certainly don't take the credit for opening the door. Thank Him for opening it. Walk in it with your head bowed and continue to be obedient. I know that God can use a small door to give me something big, and I also understand that God can bring forth a huge storm just to show me that He has a rainbow. But the point is that God is the ruler of all things and He places me where He would have me to go, and I won't move unless He moves me.

Obtain the World or Be Swallowed by It

Walk in it with your head bowed.

Those who are born of God overcome the world, and they then gain the world. This is the transition that happens where you go from being faithful over the few things, and God making you ruler over many. This is the point where your relationship makes the decision of whether you are going to obtain the world or be swallowed up by the world. Put the past behind you and take a huge step forward. God just changed your position, and you have been transitioned into ruling the things that you desired. He has given you dominion in the situation. You are born to overcome. There is nothing the enemy should be able to present to you that you can't overcome.

What's important to note is whenever you gain the world and you don't operate and handle it the way that it should be handled, then you are at risk of losing it. You have power in your hands. If you fall because of pride, you will lose your power. Then you will have to start all over with gaining the trust of God back and showing that you can have power and will not operate in pride.

When you allow pride to control your power, then you are headed toward a fall. Do not abuse God's grace just because you are standing in a position of power. Do not play with your odds because you have been placed in position. You need to know that because you have been positioned in the seat of greatness you cannot get away with the stuff that you used to get away with. When God calls you to your promise and your purpose, you can't get away with looking back and entertaining the things that are behind you because that is how you end up losing your promise.

If you get distracted, prideful, or disobedient along the way to your promise, you will ultimately fall into destruction, and you will not be able to obtain the gift that awaits you. So you must lose your fleshly self, and your past self, but you must not lose the humbleness and gratefulness that God has placed in you. God has given you the world. You are new. Old things that were of no benefit have passed away, but you get to keep the genuine heart for God that you have gained along the way in this journey.

Your position and placement are new, but your heart for God is the same. Stay true to the person God has formed within you. He's called you to this journey. You are *new!* You may have a new position, a new call, a new purpose, and you may have to walk new, speak new, be new, and even see new. But in all of that, don't lose who you are deep inside. Stay solid and stand tall in your position with excitement and passion.

What good would it be for you to have the world in your hands and then allow people to manipulate you to do what they want you to do? If you cave in to the pressure of becoming what people want you to be, you will lose and forfeit yourself.

Keep Your Heart True

Let me explain it this way. My daughter watches *Sofia the First,* the Disney Junior television series. I love that cartoon! Anyway, let me tell you a little bit about Sofia. Sofia became a princess overnight, and she had to figure out how to do things right. There was so much for her to learn and see. She got access to a mansion (castle) and she was switched out of her public school to attend a school just for royalty. She was faced with adventures, but she remained excited to be Sofia the First. She gained the world.

Her name was changed, her position was changed, her title was changed, and she gained access to the world. Everyone did whatever she asked, but Sofia's heart was compassionate. She was loving and a good friend. She was a sweet little girl at her core, and she was humble, too. She was always trying to do the right thing. Even her gifts were different than anyone else's gifts. What am I saying? Although Sofia gained the world and was able to do things no one else was able to do, she didn't lose herself. She didn't forfeit her heart for the key to the world.

You don't have to forfeit who God has created you to be in order for you to gain the desires of your heart. You are uniquely and specifically made for God's perfect purpose in you. You're a light for your generation. You may have walked through the dark areas, but because you have decided to walk with God, your life will never be the same again.

That's what our Scripture at the beginning of this chapter is all about—the ability to gain the world but not lose yourself. It's time for you to accept your position and walk in it. Stop carrying the weight of the hurt from the past. No more! God has seen you as good enough, and because of that you can walk with your head held high and not worry about the hurts of the world. Stand in your power, not your pride.

It's been a long journey and we have overcome a lot of hurdles, but God is not done with us yet. God needs to know that if He gives you what you have commanded to manifest, that you aren't going to go on a power trip. God needs to be able to trust you with the power. Perhaps that's why we aren't seeing a lot of "the sick healed and the dead raised" moments. Could it be that instead of giving God the glory for the manifestation of power we, in our arrogance, and take the credit for ourselves?

Stand in your power, not your pride.

Keep your humility close to your heart so that you always have access. You don't have to tell people that you are royalty. God will speak for you. You don't have to defend your position or placement. God has put you there. You don't have to put disclaimers out for the power that is in you, just keep walking in it. When God is operating through you, He will speak for Himself. Walk in your gift and stay humble. Give God the credit and He will take it from there.

Stay Solid

I thank God that He is moving things out of the way so people can see the gifts in you. I thank

God that you have been chosen and called to pursue and produce your purpose and promise. *May you take up your bed and walk into victory in the name of Jesus. It is so and so it is by the power of the Holy Ghost. Amen!* Whatever you do, don't lose yourself, don't lose your faith, and don't lose your hope. If you have a little bit of hope, then you have something for your faith to stand on. If the devil can take your hope, then he can take your substance.

My husband, Brandon, has coined the phrase, "Stay solid." What this means is that no matter what the devil tries to do to shake who you are and who you are called to be, stay solid. I issue this phrase to you—stay solid. Don't lose yourself in trying to gain the world, and don't then gain the world and lose yourself. Stay solid in who God has called you to be and in the end it will work out just fine.

I have found comfort in my battle with infertility because I am in God's hands, and I have truly cast my cares upon the Lord. When I was a little girl I understood the revelation of these two Scriptures:

> *No temptation has overtaken you except what is common to mankind. And God is faithful; He will not let you be tempted beyond what you can bear. But when you are tempted, He will also provide a way out so that you can endure it* (1 Corinthians 10:13 NIV).

> *Cast your cares on the Lord and He will sustain you; He will never let the righteous be shaken* (Psalm 55:22 NIV).

I understood that no matter what I am going through, God will never put more on me than I can bear. In my heart I know that I will not have anything to bear if I will cast everything on Him. He said He will sustain me. What does *sustain* mean? *Sustain* means "to strengthen or support physically or mentally." So if God is standing for me and I cast all my problems, struggles, and hurts on to God, then He will physically and mentally strengthen me and support me.

So I say to you, whatever it is that you are carrying that isn't benefiting you, cast that weight on to God. Sometimes I hear, "Man, God said He wouldn't put more on me than I can bear, but honestly this feels too heavy." The only reason it seems unbearable to you is because you haven't cast the weight on to God. You have let pride overpower you, causing you to feel like you are strong enough to handle everything on your own. So you take on the world and you lose yourself because you continue to bottle up your weight instead of casting it on to God. What would happen if you would throw all that pride and all that weight to God and you walk in liberation?

Bow Your Head and Stay Humble

Let's talk about pride for a second before we close out this chapter. *Pride* means "a feeling or deep pleasure or satisfaction derived from one's own achievements." You may have gained the world, but it wasn't through your own achievement. Your accomplishments were achieved through God and your submission to God. What is fascinating is that God is able to use us for something bigger than ourselves.

Don't stand there waiting for God to clap for you and say you have done well. How about this? You turn around and clap for God because He allowed you to achieve what you did achieve. He helped you to gain the world so that you could access power. Now that you are walking in your purpose, don't stop praising Him for it. When you have obtained your power, when you have seen the gift of the promise, don't stop thanking God because it is in your gratitude that you are given more access. You can praise Him 'til the walls come down, but after they have come down praise Him because He did it! Praise Him because He's given you access to something great.

So what's the point? You have the power—don't lose it because of pride. When the doors open, walk through humbly and stay humble. When you reach your promise, and God actually gives it to you in your hand, don't take it and run and start showing people how shiny it is before you say thank You. Don't be a spoiled, entitled brat to the King of kings. Receive your gift in full understanding that He did it and you did nothing to deserve this gift. Recognize that He didn't have to call you to your promise and give it to you.

The biblical concept is quite simple and it goes a little something like this: "Give thanks to the Lord, for His love endures forever." The way that you do not allow pride to take your power is through having a grateful heart and staying humble.

I support you wholeheartedly and I am behind you. More importantly, God is behind you. Just walk with your head bowed before the King in order for you to keep your hands on your power.

It is in your gratitude that you are given more access.

Don't look back. Stop giving the people who hurt you in your past the power that is rightfully yours. Forgive those who have hurt you—not just for them but for you. If you need help mentally, physically, emotionally, and spiritually, walk to it. There is absolutely nothing wrong with needing help to get to your power, and there is nothing wrong with being afraid to succeed. Focus on your healing, physically and mentally, and search for the support and help you need to become great.

Has God convicted you of pride as you read this chapter? Conviction is a wonderful thing! Admit your sin to God and at your request He will cleanse you. Tell God right now that you humble yourself in your own eyes and He will lift you into His glorious light. Walk in your light and walk in your call, and push people into their destiny. Pick power over pride. You are a child of the King! Let me pray for you right now.

> *I pray that your life be a representation of what God is doing in you. I pray that you don't lose the gifts and power that has been granted to you since walking through this journey. I pray that you will be able to find the light in every dark place. I pray that God will strengthen your confidence in your power and purpose. I pray that you would humble yourself and see His glory in every success that He allows you to obtain. I pray that the strongholds of peer pressure be freed off of you, and that you walk in liberation as a leader and follower of Christ. I pray that you overpower the strongholds of pride. I pray that you always maintain your power according to God's will for your life. I pray that you start feeling you are good enough to be in your position.*

> *I pray that you stop living in the consequences from your past decisions and start living in the blessings of today. I pray you thank God that you have overcome those decisions, difficulties, and dysfunctions. I pray that you are lifted and God challenges you every day to become the person He has called you to be. You are stronger than you know. The enemy is trying to distract you. I pray right now that you would resist the distractions and walk forward without looking back. May*

God bless your heart to forgive those who didn't understand you. May God bless and soften your heart so that it remains humble enough to be able to ask for forgiveness to those you have offended. I thank God for the position He has placed you in during this season. And together we humbly say, "Thank You, God, for all You've given us." Amen and amen.

Scan this code for Cora's Chapter 11
PRAYER FOR YOU!

Or Visit
WWW.CORAJAKESCOLEMAN.COM

Faithing It

CHAPTER
TWELVE

This is a BIG Deal!

Jesus looked at them and said to them,
"With men this is impossible, but with
God all things are possible."

(MATTHEW 19:26)

We've been on an amazing journey together! You're going to change this world because you are faithing it! You've surrendered, and God is proud to fight for you. God has desired your heart for so long, and at this point your purpose is ready to come forth. You have gone through the pain and the storms. You have embraced the hurt of the process so that you could make it to this moment.

I've been honored to join you in this chapter of your life's book. I've enjoyed walking together with you. I hope that after you read the last page, you walk away changed from the process we have both faced and conquered together. I pray that you are walking in purpose and accepting the changes in your life. You could have stayed where you were, but God has called you to the forefront. The power that you were always searching for is now attainable through Christ Jesus living in you, through you, and for you. Your promise, your dreams, your purpose are all about to manifest because of the power and authority you have decided to tap into. You are now officially a threat to the kingdom of hell!

When you are walking in your purpose, you are a threat to the devil and there will be many trials and tests that you have to accept and walk through. Being a threat and a powerfully positioned person in the Kingdom comes with many obstacles. You have greatness inside of you and with that comes many mountains. But guess what? If you are in relationship with God and accountable to Him, you will achieve your position over your problems. You have gained the faith to overcome it all.

God has called you to the forefront.

You Are a Gift to the Kingdom

At this point, God has given you everything that you need for your journey to purpose. He alone is your keeper and all you need to do is trust Him completely. Keep faithing it! Let's walk together in liberation from this day forward, believing God will fulfill every promise that He has given to us. Stay focused, my friend. Don't lose yourself in the journey. Continue to have a heart to serve God above all and He will have a heart to serve you. Delight yourself in the Lord, and He will give you the desires of your heart.

There is a reward in the fire. God is with you while you stand in the fire. The power is gained in your encounter with God in that fire. Go low and humble yourself so God can use you to your full capacity. Again I remind you to let go of the hurt, let go of the anger, let go of the bitterness, and walk in the freedom and power of the Holy Spirit.

You are a gift to the Kingdom, so carry yourself like the prince or princess that you are. You have the power to command that mountain to move. Speak to it with authority. Speak over your desire, declare what you want, and watch God get it for you. You are empowered to succeed!

There is a reward in the fire.

Walk in Your Authority

We hear all the time about God's ability, but we have the same authority and ability living in us. Let's not forget that God wants us to connect to the Holy Spirit and His power resting in us. You are blessed by God to have the power to manifest your purpose. Walk in it from this day forward. God has promised you the land of milk and honey, so do not look back, and do not get distracted. Walk forward. The storms and floods of life will rage, but God is bigger than every storm. He has given you the power to walk through that storm and move that mountain through your faith. Believe God and you will tap into a realm that would have never been obtainable otherwise.

More importantly, you will reach a place of power that you would have never reached had you not chosen Him.

We have the power to make the blind see, to heal the sick, and raise the dead. We are no longer carrying around the bitterness from the cross we had to carry. We know what it is to believe God over our bitterness so that He has our true self. Glory to God! I am so thankful that we have time to live another day to faith our fights and be consumed by God!

My Last Challenge to You

So here it is. This is bittersweet, but here is the last challenge you will receive in this book: I challenge you to truly believe and receive the power of the Holy Ghost within yourself. I challenge you to overcome your anger from the story and life that you had to live in the past, and believe that God is going to do something better in your future.

You have the power to walk in greatness. All you have to do now is reach up and grab it. You are amazing! There is nothing too hard for God, and with Him living in you there is nothing too hard for you. The bigger your mess, the bigger your message! God has given you something to live through so that you have a testimony.

The Power of Your Testimony

I grew up thinking of my testimony as a test. God brought me through the test of a car accident because of my need for a healing. You may be in a test, but you are healed by the lessons you learn in that test. Don't get angry, now! Allow yourself to experience the test so that you have a story.

When you are faced with a test, start faithing it. Make faithing it a moral core value where you face your day-to-day life by faith. Command joy, peace, and harmony in your day and it will come to pass. We give too much power to the enemy. Now it's time for us to take that power back. Leap forward into your purpose, and allow God to manifest through you.

All this time God wanted your heart and the broken pieces. I am so proud of who you have become, and God is proud of you for choosing Him. Continue to walk in this thing called purpose. You are born to be a winner. Hopefully, by this point in the book, you have gone from a fighter who stands alone to faithing your struggles with God. I hope that you are no longer hiding your weaknesses, but you are boasting in your weaknesses and allowing God to be the strength of your life. Hopefully you are delighting yourself in God and gaining your true heart's desire.

The bigger your mess, the bigger your message!

You Are a Faither!

You are a faither! And you will accomplish great things for God through your faith. I am grateful for the gifts in you because your gifts make room for the next generation to follow and birth their gifts. I am grateful that you've tapped into God's power. Your power will give you the key to greatness, and you will be able to give the generation behind you the key to the power within them. You are not alone, for God is with you. He is standing for you, with you, and in you, and all you have to do is open the door to receive it.

Be able to receive as well as you give, and get in a habit of loving yourself the way God would have you to be loved. You know when you are mistreating yourself and not loving yourself enough. Love you enough so that you can love others, but also allow people to love on you. You are destined for greatness, so be willing to accept yourself as God sees you. If God calls you a ruby, stop acting like a cubic zirconia! If God calls you priceless and made in His image, stop living like you aren't good enough and feeling bad for yourself.

The Father Says to You...

The Father says, "Rise up, My daughter, arise My son, and come forth into the destiny that I have prepared for you. Cast your cares on Me. I am prepared to carry your weight. Do not worry about the weights of the world—I will figure this out, and pave the way for you. Reach for what you desire and it shall be yours.

"Walk in peace, for it is yours. Don't show the enemy your doubts, show him My authority. Trust Me as you have trusted yourself. Lean on Me as you have leaned on yourself. Depend on Me as you have depended on yourself, and I will shift your mindset so that you are able to tap into the true calling and authority that rightfully belongs to you. I am that I am, and I am all that you need."

It's Time to Go!

Go to God. Give that weight to God, give that pain to God. Don't give Him a little. Don't hold back because you think you can handle it better than He can. Give Him everything. You have a friend in Jesus, and He has planted someone in your life to be a friend of wisdom and guidance in the time of need. You are not alone.

God is the producer of purpose. Let Him control things or you are going to be left outside of the building of purpose wishing that you had the guts to go in and take what's yours. And while you are standing outside of this building, people are surpassing you.

God's output will always be better than your input because He is God and God alone. Will you continue to be okay with a mediocre position and blessings? Or will you open your mind to the possibility that there is someone greater and more powerful than you? I urge you to sit down so that God can stand up. I urge you to embrace the blessings of God that have been given to you. I urge you to search for God in every storm and not even concentrate on the rain. I urge you to be a supernatural dreamer so that you can obtain supernatural blessings and dreams from God.

Don't show the enemy your doubts, show him My authority.

God claimed your promise for you before the foundations of this world. He is holding it in His hands, and when you are in your perfect spot He will place it in your hands. Stop panicking, stressing, and predicting the worst because that is not going to happen. Release yourself to the will of God, and allow Him to move in you. When God is moving in you, then you have the authority through Christ Jesus. He is still moving things in order to bless you.

I am writing to tell you that your time is not running out. God is simply positioning you, and what He said will happen, will indeed happen. You are a testimony, and your storm must match where you are going. The bigger your storm, the bigger your ministry. Don't ask God for something big and think you will have little storms. He is positioning you to His perfect will so that you can receive what you asked for.

The bigger your storm, the bigger your ministry.

I've walked the road to purpose. I've walked the road to producing my promise, and I am still walking some of those roads. So let me tell you if you didn't already know—it's not an easy road. After my father told me that I couldn't stop fighting, I heard God tell me, "Nehemiah is coming, just not yet." I wiped my tears away, and I starting faithing with all my might, with everything I had. I became a faither—and I am still a faither.

Your Purpose Is a Big Deal!

Just because the storm comes doesn't mean that the promise is delayed. Your storm is telling you that your purpose is a big deal! Your storm is telling you that your promise is a big deal! It just means God is making your breakthrough bigger.

He is positioning you to His perfect will, and it won't be easy, but you are about to win. What you have been assigned to do in the Kingdom is a *big* deal, and that's why you are going through what you are going through. You will win if you don't faint and if you let God take control.

I am a faither. I may be crying, but I am not broken. I faced my infertility both spiritually and naturally, understanding that if I want to be a producer of great things, I must take responsibility for myself. I need to say, "I'm not producing because I am afraid of what will happen if I let this all go and let God really take over." I am daily looking for God to show me what He sees in me. I am daily faithing every trial, faithing every storm, faithing every struggle. I am faithing, and guess what? You can start faithing too. It's time for you to move forward. The reason why we are faithing is because the seed that God has planted within us is a big deal!

I told you earlier that I wrote this book because I love you, and I do not want you to feel alone or be alone. I mean that. God is for you, so rest in God's ability. You are ready now, and what God has spoken for you to have will come to pass because His Word cannot come back void. The enemy may be after your faith for what God promised, but no more! You have decided to start faithing it. If God is fighting in you and through you, then you cannot lose. You are a faither!

Are you ready to fight with your faith to produce your purpose? I am praying for you and supporting you.

My heart's desire is that you overcome your past and propel into your purpose. God placed us on the earth at this time so that we can become the generation of people who shift the world for God. May

God find us standing strong for Him and preparing the path for Christ's return. My heart's desire is that you are healed and that you walk in that healing and that you soar in spirit because you are faithing it!

The seed that God has planted within us is a big deal!

From this point forward, the enemy will not control your story, your win, or your life. This is *your* time to move forward with the zeal of the Lord and fight with your faith to produce God's purpose in your life.

Go, my friend. *Go.* You have the key. God has granted you access to His purpose—all He is asking is that you trust Him, and He will supersede your expectations. My friend, your purpose awaits. It's time for you to GOOOOOOO!

Please, let's join together in a prayer of agreement this one last time.

> *I pray you have boldness now to speak to your promise to manifest. I pray that the anointing that destroys the yoke is being consumed in you. I pray that the light of God is following you in every dark place. I pray that a hedge of protection is kept around your soul, mind, and heart. May God give you the strength to overcome the struggles of life, so that you begin to embrace yourself, and who you are in God. I pray you begin to see your surroundings, and God helps you to be a leader in every atmosphere He places you in.*

*May God help you to birth your purpose like never before.
May you be a healthy producer, and may God grant you
the ability to do great works in Him. You are destined for
greatness! May you begin to walk toward that destination.
I pray peace consume the problems in your life, and God
replace the struggles of your life with strategy. I pray that you
begin to speak life instead of labels over your situations. I
pray the glory of the Lord follow and keep you all the days of
your life, and that God will begin to put the power in your
hands that you need in order to achieve what is needed in the
natural and spiritual realm.*

*I pray that your faith stand for you against the major
and minor things of life. I pray you be great in your field,
and outside of your field, and that God will grant you
supernatural understanding in your mind. I pray that the
things that used to be hard for you will now flow easily to you.
I pray that God give you the kind of mind that you need to
accomplish your purpose and that you will feel an urgency of
purpose from the very depths of your soul.*

*I thank You, God, that Your child is coming forward right
now. I thank You that the desires of their heart are being
fulfilled. I thank You, God, that this child of Yours is no
longer bound by their storms but they are now liberated in
them. I thank You, God, for the purpose that You have placed
inside of my friend, and I pray, God, that You put fire into
his heart, put fire into her heart, so they achieve their dreams
with the right mindset and goals.*

*Lord, I pray You put a thirst for You in our hearts so we don't
forget You. I pray, Lord, that You show Your glory in every
place that we ask for it. I thank You, God, that You are the
Savior of all, and that You are walking with us.*

*I pray that my friend will have the passion to finish the things
that they start, and the power to understand that they are
good enough to finish it. I love You, God, and I thank You*

for considering my friend for great purpose, and I thank You for placing the moral value of faithing into their heart. I thank You, Lord, that You are the power within us. Help us, God, to keep faithing it and to stay humble in that. I thank You, God, that You are great, and within us You will do great things, and manifest it for Your perfect glory. Amen and Amen. So be it.

EPILOGUE

It's been my honor to spend this journey with you and to share a bit of my journey and some of my friends' testimonies. You have the key to the door. Now I can't wait to see what faithing looks like on you!

God Bless You!

Your sister and friend,

Cora Jakes Coleman

Faithing It

ACKNOWLEDGMENTS

The idea of *Faithing It* was birthed from a very sensitive place within me after finding out that I wouldn't be able to birth the son I had dreamed of since I was 10 years old without fertility treatments. It hurt me, and for a long while my faith was shaken. God began to show and teach me through my battle about faith and the power of it. This is my first published book and I am so excited that God saw fit to use me as a vessel to send out His word to the people. However, just like any gift there is a large team that creates the final product before you have it in your hand. In *Faithing It* I talk to the reader (my friend) about the process. Well, I wouldn't have been able to process or produce this book without my back support—without someone believing in my message. Before we go any further into my heart for this book, I want to take time to extend my deepest thank you to the people who believed in my movement. Not just the book, but my movement of faith and bringing purpose back to life. I want to acknowledge and appreciate the people who birthed me, for without them I would not have been able to do any of this. Mommybear and Daddybear Bishop Thomas Dexter Jakes and Elder Serita Ann Jakes, you both showed me how to turn to God when I had no one else to turn to. You never let me give up on my dreams; instead, you stood behind me and fought with me. I appreciate you standing behind me; I'm a better faither because of you guys and I hope I am able to birth a stronger faith in you all from the faith you placed in me. I would also like to acknowledge my covering; the priest and prophet of my home; my lover; my king; my diary; my teacher; my minister; my heart, mind, body, and soul; my artist; my baby's father, Brandon Coleman (aka Skii Ventura)—baby, you supported me as I became closer to God. Thank you for listening to my theories, for wisdom, for holding my heart, and being my teammate. Thank you for watching our babies as I went to ministry school; thank you for caring for me when I was sick; for wiping my tears as I cried from the loss of our embryos and failed IVF cycles. Thank you for protecting me when I was scared. Thank you for loving me when I couldn't love you back. I am a better person because of you, and I acknowledge you.

Since I was young, all I ever wanted was for someone to believe in me. Someone to see my storms and say, "She has a story." I wanted someone to use my pain to help someone else to get through his or hers. Someone to turn my tears and the outcry that my soul made every time I would go through the storms of life into a message for the miserable. When I became a woman I realized my purpose to bring life to the hurting meant I would go through hurt as well, but in that I have gained a story. One day I walked into a service with my beautiful adopted blessing of a daughter Amauri when Jan Miller from the Dupree Miller Agency, whom I affectionately call my aunt, saw me and Amauri. Much to my surprise, my Mommybear would tell me later that my auntie Jan told her that when I was ready to write my story, she wanted it. There it was instantly, the one thing I wanted—someone came along. After several pitches and conversations I finally presented a blog titled Faithing It: My God Idea to my auntie Jan, and her heart instantly connected to it, and there it was she saw my book. She told me we were ready to go and she began my journey of faithing it in the publishing world. To my auntie Jan and the Dupree Miller Agency I want to say thank you for being someone to believe in my story and to want it. To Lacy Lynch, thank you for pushing my idea, connecting to it, and hopefully getting me to the *New York Times* bestsellers List. ;) I am grateful to you all for your pushing me into my purpose and believing in my legacy and continuing the legacy. Love you both.

I want to acknowledge and say thank you from the depths of my soul to all the people at Destiny Image: Don Nori, CEO; Ronda Ranalli, Publisher; Brad Herman, John Martin, Wil Brown, Sierra White, Monty Seaman—all of you believed in my movement and were willing to take a chance and make an investment of yourself and your company in someone to push and support my movement. May God send an overflow of blessings to each and every one of you. I cannot thank you enough for believing in me and investing in me. I am honored and humbled by each of you.

I want to acknowledge my Cora Jakes Coleman team—you know who you are. You interceded for me; you push me into higher levels of purpose. You believe in my gift and protect it. You help me to leap, you help me to lead, you help me to love, and you help me to be the person God called me to be. You mean more to me then you could possibly know. Thank you for covering me and my children, spiritual, adopted, and even unborn. You are the reason I don't worry about a thing and how I am able to be effective in every area of my life. I am honored and humbled to serve and be served by you.

I want to acknowledge my Potter's House family especially Zakiya Larry, Regina Lewis, Marcus Dawson, Canditha Davis, Jamel Ware, Beverly Robinson, Cammy Garner, Belinda Adams, and television production team of the Potter's House and all the other very special staff who helped to make me who I am. Thank you to those who have supported my vision and hope. Thank you for trusting me and teaching me. I'm grateful for the experiences I have had with my Potter's House Family and in the Potter's House. Thank you for never underestimating me.

I want acknowledge and say thank you to the PR team: Daniel Decker, Higher Level Group (marketing and website); Doug Hudson, Darla Lyons;and the team at The Hub (Live Events) Karen Lee, Anthony Jackson, and the team at W&W PR. You all have helped *Faithing It* move forward and be seen in the world. For the staying up all night to develop a website; for making sure the content was what I wanted. Thank you for believing in my image and putting me in the best light. Thank you for giving me a voice and respecting it.

I want to acknowledge and say thank you to those of you who have cheered me on and joined my movement. You cannot have success without someone to cheer you on and to love you enough to sacrifice of themselves and of their testimony to join your faithing it movement and be a part of it by sharing their gifts to make your movement even greater. So to my friend Livre, for writing the anthem to my book and providing a worship experience to the faithers out there trying to overcome their obstacles; to my close friends Monet Cullins and Michelle Loud, who have started their *Faithing It* journey and trusted me with your gifts and purpose—I say thank you, and I am so proud of you.

Last but not least, thank you to those who have endorsed my movement, both nationally and locally. Thank you to my family for supporting me and having my back. Thank you to my sisters and brothers for praying for me and covering me in prayer. Jamar Jakes, my oldest brother, thank you for sharing wisdom with me as a child and then being an example of that. Jermaine Jakes, thank you for trusting me with your heart and destiny, always pushing me to pray and receiving my wisdom even as my oldest brother. Sarah Jakes Robert (Sissy), thank you for being my best friend, for being closer to me then I am to myself, for being my person, protecting me, healing me, and giving me the inspiration to use my pain to help someone else. Not sure if you knew this, but you healed me by healing yourself through the faith you walk in daily. I am so glad you have true love and joy; may God propel you and your enemies be scattered. Thank you for always coming when I needed you the most. I love you. To Dexter Jakes, thank you, baby brother, for your care for never judging me, for always having a joke when I needed it. Thank you for being there. I am so proud of the young man you have become. I can't wait to see the nation get an opportunity to see what I see. I love you all; you mean the world to me.

To my friends, followers, and people who have shared my ministry, I acknowledge you; and last, because what is last shall be first, I acknowledge God for placing a purposed seed in me, for giving me the gift to speak life and understanding and bring about breakthrough. You are my father, my friend, you are everything to me, and I acknowledge you for every step I take from here forward. Have your way in my life and breathe life into this movement and into this book. Amen.

Faithing It

ABOUT THE AUTHOR

For more information about the author visit
www.corajakescoleman.com

Faithing It

GROUP LEADER OUTLINES

Purposeful Pain

Cora Jakes Coleman

Key Scriptures:

For it was fitting that He, for whom and by whom all things exist, in bringing many sons to glory, should make the founder of their salvation perfect through suffering. For He who sanctifies and those who are sanctified all have one source. That is why he is not ashamed to call them brothers, saying, "I will tell of Your name to my brothers; in the midst of the congregation I will sing Your praise." And again, "I will put my trust in Him." And again, "Behold, I and the children God has given me."
(Hebrews 2:10-13 ESV)

And the LORD restored the fortunes of Job, when he had prayed for his friends. And the LORD gave Job twice as much as he had before. Then came to him all his brothers and sisters and all who had known him before, and ate bread with him in his house. And they showed him sympathy and comforted him for all the evil that the LORD had brought upon him. And each of them gave him a piece of money and a ring of gold. And the Lord blessed the latter days of Job more than his beginning. And he had 14,000 sheep, 6,000 camels, 1,000 yoke of oxen, and 1,000 female donkeys. He had also seven sons and three daughters.
(Job 42:10-13 ESV)

Introduction:
You have been saved into a life of victory. As we go through the storms and pain of life, we must live mindful that victory is God's ultimate destination for us, not just in heaven, but on earth. A victory perspective helps us to see purpose in the pain that we go through.

A. You Have Been Saved

1. Your former status. We who have been in sin—uncleansed, broken vessels, shamed, embarrassed, crushed, humiliated—have felt like we can't go to God.

2. Your life-changing decision. Those of us who have decided to step into the calling and chosen the legacy of the power of God need to understand that we will face death, and death isn't enjoyable. Dying to yourself, spiritually, naturally, and or otherwise, is painful.

3. Your redeemed position. When we make the step toward God, we receive the work of Jesus, the One who stepped in and took our punishment. Because of His work, we have been saved.

4. Your new enemy. When you embrace your position in Christ, the enemy will come in like a flood against you. Just remember that God promised that the flood would never destroy you (see Isa. 43:2; 59:19).

B. You are Victorious

1. You are consumed by Christ. The simple fact that you choose to be consumed by Christ means that you have conquered the enemy.

   You are clothed in Christ—the One who defeated and conquered the enemy (see Gal. 3:27; Rom. 13:14).

2. Jesus' victory is your victory.

3. You need to have a victory perspective—think from a perspective of victory.

4. If the enemy can tap into your mentality, he can control your movement: Your thoughts dictate your life.

Stop being afraid of the storm when you are walking in Christ.
You have been given the power to calm the storm...
and rest in the storm!

KEYS TO SEEING THE PURPOSE IN YOUR PAIN

Pain Provides Opportunity for God's Power to Be Displayed

A. God Has Placed His Power in You

1. Jesus died so you could live. You are both crucified in Christ and raised up with Christ (Gal. 2:20).

2. You are dead to sin and alive to God in Christ Jesus (Rom. 6:2,11).

3. You laid down your old life as a bound sinner, so you could pick up His resurrection life and power.

4. The same Spirit that raised Jesus from the dead lives inside of you.

5. All of this shows how passionate God was about saving you, so you could be filled with His power.

B. God Has a Purpose for the Power in You

1. The Bible says that the Son of God was made manifest to "destroy the works of the devil" (1 John 3:8).

2. Jesus lives in you and through you because of the Holy Spirit.

3. This means that you—the church—are the body of people charged to destroy the works of the enemy.

4. One of these works is the spirit of fear.

   For God hath not given us the spirit of fear; but of power, and of love, and of a sound mind (2 Timothy 1:7 KJV).

5. Start with you! Shift your mentality, take your power back, and say "NO" to the spirit of fear that is trying to overwhelm your life.

C. Testing Develops and Releases the Power in You

1. Presence of the Tests

   Tests are a normal part of life, and no one is exempt—even Jesus! (See Psalm 105:19.)
   Jesus was tested and tempted by the devil.

You will be tested and tempted as well.

2. **Passing the Tests**

   Jesus passed the test of the enemy by declaring the Word of God (See Matthew 4:7).

   You have access to the same Word, the same truth and the same promises that Jesus did when He overcame the enemy in the wilderness.

3. **Purpose of the Tests**

   After the wilderness temptation, Jesus began His ministry that changed the course of history.

   Your test is going to propel you into your ministry—helping *others* pursue and discover their purpose!

   Everything you learn from your test, you can share with others and help them pass their tests in life.

4. **Lessons from the Tests**

   The tests teach us patience (See Hebrews 3:8).

   Patience positions us for endurance.

   Endurance is key to receiving our victory and breakthrough—we cannot give up, no matter how difficult the test or how fierce the storm.

   On the other side of our endurance is His victory.

5. **Declarations in the Tests**

   During the tests of life, we need to remind ourselves of Truth Anchors: Unchanging realities that will keep us grounded.

   a. We are more than conquerors in Christ (see Rom. 8:37)!

   b. Greater is He who lives in me than he who is in the world, and against me (see 1 John 4:4)!

   c. I am passing through the valley of the shadow of death—I won't die there (see Ps. 23:4)!

   d. Suffering won't kill me; it will strengthen me!

   e. I am anointed by the Holy Spirit and with power to have victory over every work of the enemy (see 1 John 3:8; Luke 10:19)!

God's power brings healing where there is brokenness.

God's power provides miracles where there are impossible situations.

God's power releases solutions to the problems of pain.

Pain is the Process of Perfection: Suffering

A. Suffering Produces Perfection

1. Perfect is defined as something that is complete, whole or without blemish (see Prov. 17:3).

2. Crushing leads to completion (see James 1:3).

3. You cannot get to completion if you aren't willing to suffer the crushing.

4. You are not perfect in your own humanity, but you are made perfect in your willingness to walk in Christ, with Christ, and for Christ.

5. You are living out your identity as someone who is "in Christ."

B. Suffering Builds Endurance

1. Endurance is defined as: "*The fact or power of enduring an unpleasant or difficult process or situation without giving way.*"

C. Suffering Ends in Wholeness

1. In order for God to be our Healer, and to bring about wholeness to us, He had to first be willing to enter our broken vessel; something we inhabit (see 1 Pet. 1:7).

2. In order for God to heal, there needs to be a malady and an issue for which He can release His healing.

D. Suffering Positions You for Success

1. Sometimes you will have to go through the tests just to get to an encounter with Jesus.

2. It is the encounter with Jesus that can make you whole. The greatest example of this is when we first come to embrace Jesus as Lord and Savior.

3. Because Jesus stepped into a broken vessel and redeemed us, we are able to walk in righteousness (see Col. 1:14).

4. Even though you experienced great suffering before Jesus came into your life—the sins of your past, the hurt of your past, the brokenness, the fear of failure, the fear of success—God laid all of this suffering on Jesus, on your behalf, to bear on the Cross.

5. Jesus' suffering positions you for success (Define success).

Forgiveness from your sins, past, and shame.

Right standing with God.

Power over the enemy.

It is time for you to start walking in the power that Jesus paid for!

E. Jesus' Presence in Your Pain

1. God is groaning with you. God isn't just idly watching you groaning in your pain; Scripture says that He joins us in our groaning.

> *Likewise the Spirit helps us in our weakness. For we do not know what to pray for as we ought, but the Spirit Himself intercedes for us with groanings too deep for words* (Romans 8:26 ESV).

2. Jesus is making intercession for you. He is not just watching you pray, but the Bible says He is seated at the Father's right hand, making intercession for you.

> *Who then is the one who condemns? No one. Christ Jesus who died--more than that, who was raised to life--is at the right hand of God and is also interceding for us* (Romans 8:34 NIV).

> *He always lives to intercede for them* (Hebrews 7:25 NIV).

3. Jesus did not forsake you or forget you; He allowed you to go through all the storms and all of the pain in order for you to receive the double portion.

> *Instead of your shame there shall be a double portion.* (Isaiah 61:7 ESV).

Conclusion:

If you aren't willing to face the real you– the broken vessel—and if you aren't willing to expose your vulnerability to the Man that revealed His naked self to the world for the very idea of you, how will you propel?

A. Get Real with God

1. How will you gain the process and lesson in the pain if you aren'twilling to have a relationship with the Teacher?

    a. It's okay to be vulnerable with God.

    b. It's okay to be smelly with God.

    c. It's okay to come to God shattered.

    d. It's okay to come to God torn, bleeding, and feeling forsaken.

2. Jesus had to be willing to risk His body in order to save His body.

> *...looking unto Jesus, the author and finisher of our faith, who for the joy that was set before Him endured the cross, despising the shame, and has sat down at the right hand of the throne of God* (Hebrews 12:2, NKJV).

    a. The testing is hard.

    b. There is a crushing in the testing.

    c. There is a crucifying in the testing.

    d. There is a fight in the testing.

    e. There is pain, backstabbing, and betrayal.

    f. There is disappointment in the testing.

B. Persevere and Be Victorious

1. But when you have passed the test, you will have grown in perseverance, and *the trials of the enemy will be of no effect.*

2. When God helps, He doesn't just help—He heals!

    a. He healed with the nails in His hands and feet.

    b. He healed with a crown of thorns on His head.

    c. He healed, being hung on a cross, naked before His own mother.

3. Because of His life, because of His willingness to step in on your behalf, you are free and can come out strong!

Jesus died for your purpose—how dare you not pursue it!

There may be pain, but it is purposeful pain and you were created to endure!

Faithing It

GROUP LEADER OUTLINES

The Ineffective Storm

Cora Jakes Coleman

Key Scripture:

> *"On that day, when evening had come, He said to them, "Let us go across to the other side." And leaving the crowd, they took Him with them in the boat, just as He was. And other boats were with Him. And a great windstorm arose, and the waves were breaking into the boat, so that the boat was already filling. But He was in the stern, asleep on the cushion. And they woke Him and said to Him, "Teacher, do you not care that we are perishing?" And He awoke and rebuked the wind and said to the sea, "Peace! Be still!" And the wind ceased, and there was a great calm. He said to them, "Why are you so afraid? Have you still no faith?" And they were filled with great fear and said to one another, "Who then is this, that even the wind and the sea obey Him?"* (Mark 4:35-41 ESV)

Introduction: The Storm's Setup

There will inevitably be storms along your journey of purpose.

It is important for you to first understand the context of this storm situation. Where were Jesus and the disciples going? They were headed to deal with demonic possession, and, on the way, they were hit by an unexpected storm. If you are called to set captives free, you yourself will face opposition. You will face trials and tribulations—this is because the enemy doesn't want you to set people free. (See 2 Corinthians 10:3-4.)

A. It wasn't the releasing of the demons that brought opposition; opposition came to try and thwart Jesus and the disciples from ever getting to the other side and bringing freedom to the captive demoniac.

B. Opposition comes on your way to experiencing and releasing breakthrough.

C. Storms are intended to try and thwart your breakthrough and miracle—especially when you are intent on bringing freedom to other people.

D. When you have the key to freedom in your hands, you will be faced with the enemy.

E. The question is: Will the storm be effective or ineffective? The storm is trying to set you up for defeat and failure. You need to choose to render its power ineffective!

Keys to Navigating Through the Storms of Life

A. Sometimes, you have to leave the crowd behind in order to walk in the direction God tells you to go.

   1. The disciples left the crowd and followed Jesus (see Matt. 8:22).

   2. They were going in an uncommon direction.

   3. Jesus is likewise inviting you into an uncommon direction, where you will leave the crowd and walk in His direction.

   4. Walking in God's direction does not come without storms.

B. God will send you into storms—fully prepared.

   1. Whether the disciples knew it or not, they were fully prepared to overcome the storm; whether you know it or not, you have everything you need to navigate through storms and come out victoriously (see 1 John 5:4).

   2. You may not feel prepared for the storm coming against you, but the All-Knowing One is your light. (see John 1:5).

   3. God sent the disciples into the direction of the storm itself, not to put them in danger, but to test their faith.

   4. They were fully prepared to render the storm ineffective, as Jesus was right there in the midst of them, and this same Jesus had authorized them to do something about the storm.

5. Jesus is with you, and He has given you authority over the storms that come against you.

C. Know who is on your boat.

1. Everybody can't be in the boat with you during a storm; however, it is very important to be surrounded by key people who call your faith up and out, not down. (See Roman. 1:12.)

2. The disciples were fortunate, whether they knew it or not, because they had each other—to build each other's faith up—and above all, they had Jesus.

    a. They should have encouraged one another to exercise their faith; but, instead, they all feared. Fear is contagious, but so is faith.

    b. They should have been more mindful of the presence of Jesus in their midst, as well.

3. They were being beaten by the waves and winds of the storm; all the while, Jesus was resting in the back of the boat.

D. Jesus is Resting in the Back of the Boat

1. Jesus is not moved or shaken by the storm you are going through.

2. His heart of compassion goes out to you, yes. (See Mark11:41.)

3. However, He is not threatened or worried by the storm coming against you.

4. Jesus knows who you are; and, more importantly, He knows Who He is in you!

5. It was not the storm itself that woke Jesus up; it was the desperate cries coming from His friends.

E. Resist Unbelief and Fear

1. Unbelief and fear can make you forget the power of your placement.

2. If we try and control what God has planned for us, it will lead to confusion. (See Proverb. 3:5.)

3. When your steps are ordered by the Lord, you have the ability to calm the storm inside of you and around you— following His steps gives you confidence.

4. The disciples were afraid of the power of the storm, because they did not fully understand the power of their faith.

    a. Your faith, no matter how small, has the power to release the peace of God.

    b. Your unbelief lies in your fear of trusting God in a situation that seems uncontrollable.

    c. How do you deal with fear?

        i. Speak to your fears to silence them.

        ii. Speak to the faith to release it.

If faith the size of a mustard seed can move a mountain, why do you think your faith couldn't move a wave?

How to Activate Your Faith in the Middle of Your Storms

Jesus addresses the *faith* of the disciples in the boat, which tells us that faith has the power to calm the storm. **Your faith has the power to calm the storm!**

A. You have the power to speak to a thing and it be still. So, why are you frightened? Start speaking to your storms! (See Romans 12:6.)

B. Don't fear. If you are facing the storms of life from a place of fear, then you have then deactivated your faith.

C. Consider Jesus' Example. The importance in this story is not just the disciples having little faith, but also in knowing who their teacher is—the Man resting in the back of the boat. They knew to wake Him up if they were in fear. Jesus was resting in the middle of the storm; they should have been following His example.

D. Jesus' rebuke reminds us of what to do in storms. Jesus' reaction to the disciples seems like a strange situation, as one would assume that the right response from the disciples would be coming to Jesus—like they did. Yet, Jesus rebuked them for a lack of faith. The truth is, Jesus had given them authority over all the works of the enemy; this same Jesus has given us authority!

E. Start using your faith! God gave you the key to victory when He gave you faith; you are not using faith independently of God—you are activating the very faith of God—the faith that God Himself deposited into your life to bring about God-sized results and breakthroughs.

I want to challenge you today to stop running to God in fear of the storm, and start exercising the power of your faith!

If your boat represents your life, and the storms represent the real threat of your life heading towards purpose, then you must first realize if God Himself didn't worry in the storms of life, why should you?

If the disciples had understood the power of their faith, they would have spoken to the elements, brought peace by faith, and gone to sleep—*just like Jesus.*

CONCLUSION: Release the Power of Your Faith!

A. **Don't run in fear.** Jesus prepared to sleep at the bottom of the boat knowing there was going to be a chaotic storm. What have you prepared for in the face of your storm? *Are you running in terror or able to sleep through it by faith?*

B. **Don't be impacted by the impact.** Just because Jesus was asleep at the back of the boat did not mean that He didn't feel the tossing of the boat and impact of the storm. It didn't mean He didn't hear the disciples running around in fear. *Jesus simply chose not to be impacted by the impact of the storm.*

C. **Don't be surprised by the storm.** This goes to show, that if you have made a decision to walk in freedom, or to set captives free, there is a level of chaos that comes with that choice—and you can choose to rest or choose to run.

D. **Deprive the storm of its ability to hold you back!** The sooner you realize that the storms are not affecting you—they are just distracting you from your purpose—and if you keep walking forward in faith, you will get to your destination.

Just remember what Jesus said to the disciples:

"Let us go across to the other side." (Mark. 4:3, ESV).

He is saying the same to you today!

I challenge you: Do not be affected by an ineffective storm!

Prayer shouldn't be a boring religious exercise.

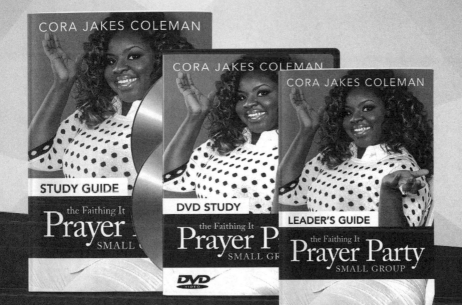

Faithing It
Prayer Party!
SMALL GROUP STUDY

COMING SOON

The *Faithing It: Prayer Party* is your opportunity to come together with others, build relationships, play games, laugh, cry, share a meal… and learn how to pray with confidence and power! Prayer doesn't have to be a boring religious activity. You can have a fun and powerful prayer party!

The *Faithing It: Prayer Party* kit includes:
Study Guide • DVD Study • Leader's Guide

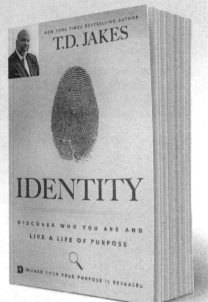